MathsBeat

Year 1
Teacher's Handbook

Mike Askew

Robert Wilne

Helen Laflin

Debbie Streatfield

Janine Blinko

OXFORD

UNIVERSITY PRESS

Great Clarendon Street, Oxford, OX2 6DP, United Kingdom

Oxford University Press is a department of the University of Oxford. It furthers
the University's objective of excellence in research, scholarship, and education by
publishing worldwide. Oxford is a registered trade mark of Oxford University Press
in the UK and in certain other countries

British Library Cataloguing in Publication Data
Data available

9780198435570

10 9 8 7 6 5 4 3 2 1

Paper used in the production of this book is a natural, recyclable product made
from wood grown in sustainable forests. The manufacturing process conforms to
the environmental regulations of the country of origin.

Printed in Great Britain by Ashford Colour Press

Acknowledgements
Written and developed by Mike Askew, Robert Wilne, Helen Laflin, Debbie
Streatfield and Janine Blinko

Cover illustrations: vectoriart/iStockphoto

Photographs by Emma Lowndes, except: pages 29 (bottom), 44, 47, 93, 94, 126, 127,
130, 131, 132, 134 and 135 by Earl Smith.

With special thanks to: Bickley Primary School, Bromley; Deer Park School,
Richmond-upon-Thames; Halley House School, London; Oaks Primary Academy,
Kent; Pickhurst Infant Academy, West Wickham; St Lawrence CE Primary School,
Alton; Sundridge and Brasted C of E Primary School, Sundridge.

Although we have made every effort to trace and contact all copyright holders
before publication this has not been possible in all cases. If notified, the publisher
will rectify any errors or omissions at the earliest opportunity.

Links to third party websites are provided by Oxford in good faith and for
information only. Oxford disclaims any responsibility for the materials contained in
any third party website referenced in this work.

MathsBeat Year 1 Teacher's Handbook

Contents

1. Number and place value
Strand overview 7
Progression through the National Curriculum 8
Tasks in practice 10

2. Addition and subtraction
Strand overview 29
Progression through the National Curriculum 30
Tasks in practice 32

3. Multiplication and division
Strand overview 51
Progression through the National Curriculum 52
Tasks in practice 54

4. Fractions
Strand overview 73
Progression through the National Curriculum 74
Tasks in practice 76

5. Geometry: properties of shapes
Strand overview 89
Progression through the National Curriculum 90
Tasks in practice 92

6. Measurement
Strand overview 105
Progression through the National Curriculum 106
Tasks in practice 108

7. Geometry: position and direction
Strand overview 127
Progression through the National Curriculum 128
Tasks in practice 130

MathsBeat Year 1 Teacher's Handbook

MathsBeat is a digitally-led resource to support teaching for mastery, crafted by teachers who understand the challenges of teaching within a UK classroom. At the heart of *MathsBeat* is the desire to make maths more available to more children. This has driven the way we've developed the *MathsBeat* materials and our thinking about the teaching sequence.

Two principles have been used throughout the programme:

1. Mathematical thinking is a natural human ability that all children can do by solving problems. Through learning maths, we can teach children to find the most efficient ways to solve problems.

2. No two classrooms are the same. *MathsBeat* provides progression with built-in flexibility and regular formative assessment support, so teachers can choose to spend longer on a task or decide that their children are ready to move on. By using the sequences of carefully designed learning tasks, children will develop knowledge, fluency, reasoning and understanding.

As part of our development work, we asked our community of teachers to trial tasks from the *MathsBeat* Digital Planner. Their experiences informed developments to the tasks themselves and were also collated to form this professional development handbook based on real classroom experience.

One of the unique features of *MathsBeat* is that it's designed to be used in a structured yet flexible way. This handbook aims to encourage that flexibility. Importantly, when trialling tasks in classrooms within our teaching community, we captured children's misconceptions and teachers' responses, resulting in the wealth of coaching support provided in the handbook. So while it has progression and formative assessment built in, *MathsBeat* importantly recognizes that only teachers can decide when their children need to spend a bit longer working on something and when they are ready to move onto the next task. In this way, every child can be at the heart of learning maths and develop the depth of learning they need.

Acknowledgements

We would like to thank all the teachers and children who have trialled our tasks, given us feedback and contributed to ideas and suggestions. Special thanks go to Bickley Primary School, Bromley; Deer Park School, Richmond-upon-Thames; Halley House School, London; Oaks Primary Academy, Kent; Pickhurst Infant Academy, West Wickham; St Lawrence CE Primary School, Alton; Sundridge and Brasted C of E Primary School, Sundridge.

About the Series Editors

Mike Askew is an internationally renowned expert in Primary mathematics education who believes that all children can act as mathematicians, given rich, engaging and challenging problems to reason about. He has taught at all levels, including teacher professional development, and led research projects throughout the world. He now researches, speaks and writes about teaching and learning mathematics. Mike believes that all children can find mathematical activity engaging and enjoyable and therefore develop the confidence in their ability to do maths.

Robert Wilne co-led the initial National Centre for Excellence in the Teaching of Mathematics (NCETM) England-Shanghai teacher exchanges, supporting Maths Hubs as they introduced teaching for mastery. He has over 20 years' experience teaching primary and secondary maths and works regularly in schools coaching and training maths teachers and developing curriculum resources.

Our teaching community

MathsBeat has been created alongside a community of teachers who have been involved at every stage of development. These teachers bring with them experience of a variety of different school types, from 3-form entry, inner-city schools to small rural schools with mixed-aged classes and from 2% to 80% English as an Additional Language (EAL). The teachers range from newly-qualified teachers to established practitioners, from classroom teachers to subject leaders, and have a variety of experience of maths mastery, to ensure that our teacher community reflects the diversity of classrooms across the United Kingdom.

At each stage, their feedback has led us to evolve the content to make sure it is fit for purpose and has an impact in schools. Through this trialling of content in classrooms across the country, we collated the authentic photographs and conversations that form this handbook.

Recruiting a teacher panel to help develop a mastery programme for every child

Valuable feedback at every stage of development

Trialling resources in the classroom to ensure they really work

An online community of users and experts to give you support and guidance

Our teaching community can be found on Facebook, where you can go to for practical tips and advice from your peers, as well as the expert author team.

Chapter 1
Number and place value

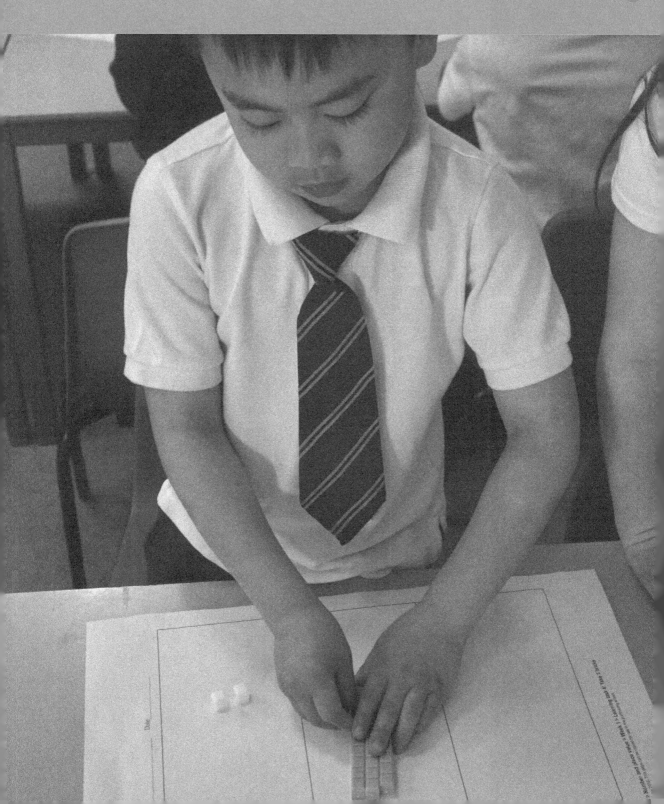

Strand overview

Aims

Children reason about how the position (place) of a digit in a numeral determines its value (worth). They solve problems involving estimating, counting and recording quantities. They develop fluency in skip counting in ones, twos, fives and tens and reason about how this is linked to adding.

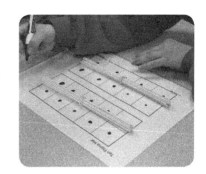

Key ideas

- The number tagged to the last object in a collection tells us the total quantity. It does not matter in which order we count the objects.

- When counting on, on a number track, we count from the next square, not the one you are on. When counting on, on a number line, we count the jumps being made, not the marks on the line.

- Children will need plenty of experience of putting numerals on number tracks and number lines to understand that each counting number has a unique position on the line.

- Children need to be exposed to the idea that partitioning a number can be done in a variety of ways (e.g. 45 can be partitioned into 4 tens and 5 ones, or 3 tens and 15 ones, or 1 ten and 35 ones and so on).

- Plenty of experience of estimating quantities before counting them to check helps develop children's number sense.

- Developing understanding of place value is based in practical experiences, not just labelling and manipulating symbols. Children need lots of experience of enumerating (establishing the total in) large collections by making groups of ten and then counting these in tens.

Models and apparatus

Developing a sound understanding of place value requires working with a wide variety of representations, including collections of real objects, 10-frames, base-ten apparatus, 10p and 1p coins, number tracks, 100-squares and number lines. When counting collections of real objects, small bowls are helpful for putting groups of ten items into.

 View the video on the Year 1 Teacher Support area of the Digital Planner

Progression through the National Curriculum

EYFS

- Have an understanding of number to 10, linking names of numbers, numerals, their value, and their position in the counting order.

- Subitize (recognize quantities without counting) up to 5.

Year 1

- Count to and across 100, forwards and backwards, beginning with 0 or 1, or from any given number.

- Count, read and write numbers to 100 in numerals; count in multiples of twos, fives and tens.

- Given a number, identify one more and one less.

- Identify and represent numbers using objects and pictorial representations including the number line, and use the language of: equal to, more than, less than (fewer), most, least.

- Read and write numbers from 1 to 20 in numerals and words.

Year 2

- Count in steps of 2, 3, and 5 from 0, and in tens from any number, forward and backward.

- Recognize the place value of each digit in a 2-digit number (tens, ones).

- Identify, represent and estimate numbers using different representations, including the number line.

- Compare and order numbers from 0 up to 100; use <, > and = signs.

- Read and write numbers to at least 100 in numerals and in words.

- Use place value and number facts to solve problems.

Year 1 sub-objectives

Term 1
- Count to 100, forwards, beginning with 0 or 1, or from any given number.
- Count from 100, backwards.
- Count, read and write numbers to 100 in numerals.
- Given a number, identify one more.
- Given a number, identify one less.
- Identify and represent numbers using objects and pictorial representations including the number track.

Term 2
- Count to and across 100, forwards, beginning from any given number.
- Count back from any given number up to 100.
- Count in multiples of twos, fives and tens.
- Given a number, identify one more.
- Given a number, identify one less.
- Identify and represent numbers using objects and pictorial representations including the number line.
- Use the language of: equal to, more than, less than (fewer), most, least.
- Read and write numbers from 1 to 20 in words.

Term 3
- Count to and across 100, forwards, beginning from any given number.
- Count back from any given number up to 100.
- Identify and represent numbers using objects and pictorial representations, including the number line.
- Use the language of: equal to, more than, less than (fewer), most, least.
- Read and write numbers from 1 to 20 in words.
- Given a number, identify one less.
- Given a number, identify one less.

Tasks in Practice

Learning task 2: Within 20

(DP) Year 1 > Term 1 > Unit 1 > Number and place value > Week 1 > Learning task 2

In this task, children model and connect different representations of the 'teen' numbers using bundles of straws, bead strings and 10-frames.

On track

Children who are 'on track' represent teen numbers as a unit of one full ten and some more ones on 10-frames.

The teacher shows a bundle of 10 straws and 2 single straws.

T: So, what have we got here with our straws?

C: *Ten here. Two here.*

T: Can you make this on your 10-frame?

(Child makes ten dots in their first 10-frame and then makes a single dot in their second 10-frame.)

T: OK. So, we have ten here and one here. Do we need any more? Look at the straws.

> Do you know how many that is altogether?

> Does the number on your 10-frame match the number of straws?

▲ Are you sure there are only 11?

(Child adds another dot to their second 10-frame.)

T: Lovely. Now we've got ten and how many ones?

C: *Twelve.*

T: We've got twelve altogether but we've got one full ten and how many more ones?

C: *Two. Ten add two equals twelve.*

T: Good. We have two ones. Can you write the number?

(Child writes 12.)

> How does working with two representations deepen understanding?

> How could place value cards support children in writing teen numbers?

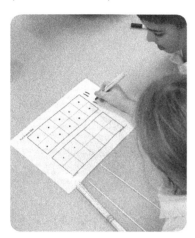

▲ How many straws are there?
Can you show this on your 10-frames?

What next?

Children talk about the pattern of the 1 to 10 numbers when looking at the 'teen' numbers. What might happen to the pattern if we carry on beyond twenty?

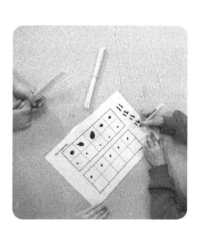

Needing support

Look and listen for children who muddle the counting sequence 10–20, e.g. counting 10, 11, 12, 30, 40, 50, 60, 70 and those who do not identify a bundle as 10 straws. Look and listen for children who represent numbers incorrectly on the 10-frames, e.g. not filling up one full 10-frame first.

The teacher shows a bundle of 10 straws and 7 single straws.

T: How many here?

C: *One?*

T: How many tens have we got? Think about ten (teacher shows bundle of ten) **and one** (teacher shows one straw). How many tens?

C: *One.*

T: Good. One ten. Could you hand me ten ones? That's ten straws.

(Children count straws together in ones to 10.)

T: Good, so we bundle these up. How many ones have I got? Can we count?

(Children count the straws together.)

T: So what number does it make? Can you count?

C: *I counted in my head.*

T: What did you count in your head?

C: *Two, four, six, eight, ten, twelve, fourteen, sixteen, seventeen.*

T: You counted in twos did you? How many tens do we have?

(Teacher holds up the one bundle of 10 straws.)

C: *One ten.*

T: So, can we count from ten? Ten (teacher raises bundle of 10 straws), **eleven** ...

(Teacher holds up the individual 7 straws one by one. Children join in the count to 17.)

▲ Ask children to count out 10 straws so they can see that a bundle is 10 ones, or 1 ten.

How could we make clear to this child that 10 ones are equal to a unit of 1 ten?

What could help children realize that counting in tens might be more efficient?

T: Good, so ten and seven makes?

C: *Seventeen.*

T: Yes, good. Can you write it?

(Child writes 71.)

T: Remember we write the tens first. It's a bit confusing isn't it, because we say 'seventeen' but we don't write the seven first.

(Child writes 17.)

T: Good. So, if I took one away, what would I have?

(Teacher takes away one straw.)

C: *Sixteen?*

T: Good. Shall we check? So, ten (teacher raises bundle of 10 straws), eleven ...

(They count together to 16.)

T: Good! Now shall we show this on our 10-frames?

(Child fills a 10-frame with dots, then adds 9 single dots to a second 10-frame, showing 19. Teacher places the 16 straws by the 10-frames.)

T: Do the 10-frames and straws match?

C: *Ten here and ten here* (child counts single dots on 10-frame and single straws) *but there are more dots than I need here!*

T: Right. So, what do we need to do?

C: *Rub some off.*

(Child counts 6 dots on the second 10-frame and rubs off 3.)

C: *Now it's right.*

Use a sentence frame and numeral cards.

____ ten and ____ ones.

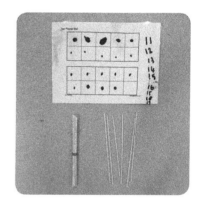

▲ Count the single straws again. Does the number of straws match what you have shown on your 10-frames?

What next?

Place completed 10-frames under each number 1–20 as children count forwards and backwards. Show children numbers written as words so they can see the 'teen' ending and emphasize 'teen' when counting aloud.

Going deeper

Show children 'teen' numbers with straws, 10-frames or on the bead string very briefly (less than 3 seconds). They confidently say how many and what might happen to the pattern if we carry on beyond 20.

The teacher briefly shows 21 with straws: two bundles of 10 and one single straw.

T: What number is this?

C: *Twenty-one.*

T: Twenty-one. Can you write twenty-one?

(Child writes 21.)

T: Can you show twenty-one using 10-frames?

(Children fill two 10-frames with dots, then add a single dot to a third 10-frame. Teacher places the two bundles of 10 straws on the filled 10-frames, and the single straw in a plastic cup.)

T: Good job. Then if we add one more straw? We've got ...?

C: *Twenty-two.*

(Teacher adds another straw to the cup. Children write 22 and add another dot to the 10-frame.)

T: Does everybody agree?

Cs: *Yes.*

T: Can you add another straw?

(Children add another straw to the cup.)

C: *Twenty-three.*

T: Can you count to check?

C: *Ten, twenty, twenty-one, twenty-two, twenty-three.*

(Children touch the bundles of straws and single straws as they count.)

T: Good. So, if you know it is twenty-two and one more, can you count on one from twenty-two?

C: *Yes. Twenty-two ... twenty-three.*

> How did you know the answer so quickly?

> Can you describe what you've shown here on your 10-frames?

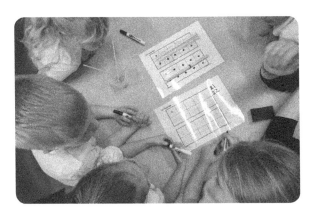

▲ There are twenty-two straws plus one more. Can you write the new number and show it on your 10-frames?

(Teacher takes one straw back out of the cup to leave 2, then holds up 3 straws.)

T: Good. What is twenty-two and three more?

C: *Twenty-two … twenty-three, twenty-four, twenty-five.*

What is the value of having the concrete present but not actually using it?

▲ Children add dots to their 10-frames and write numbers as they count.

What next?

Children work in pairs. One child makes a number using straws and shows it quickly. Can their partner show this on the 10-frame and write the number? What if I added three more straws? What if I took away two straws?

Tasks in Practice

Learning task 2: Number tracks and squares

DP Year 1 > Term 2 > Unit 7 > Number and place value >
Week 1 > Learning task 2

In this task, children make sections of a number track and assemble these into 1–100 tracks and squares.

On track

Children who are 'on track' use a 100-square to help them count fluently forward in tens from any single digit.

Children have made number tracks and assembled them into a 100-square.

T: Can you put your counter on sixteen for me?

(Child does so.)

T: And then, can you tell me, what is ten more than sixteen?

C: *Twenty-six?*

(Child points to 26 on the 100-square.)

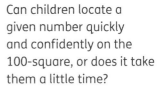

Can children locate a given number quickly and confidently on the 100-square, or does it take them a little time?

Can children immediately say the number ten more than a given number, or do they count on in ones to find the answer?

▲ Twenty-six is ten more than sixteen.

T: And what would ten more than that be?

C: *Thirty-six.*

T: And can you count on in tens for me from there?

C: *Forty-six, fifty-six, sixty-six, seventy-six.*

(Child moves their finger down the column as they say the numbers.)

T: Brilliant.

How will you know when children are confident in counting on in tens, and no longer need the 100-square for support?

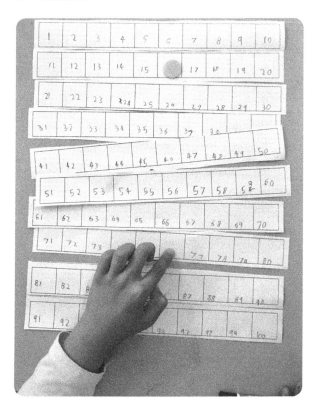

What next?

Children choose any number on the 100-square and count on in tens. What patterns do you see in the numbers? What is the same and what is different with each jump? Children cover their 100-squares. Can they still count on in tens from a given number? Children move on to counting back in tens, with and without the 100-square.

Needing support

Look and listen for children who, when counting on in ones on a 100-square, start the count on the square that they are on, not the next square. For example, they have circled 4 and start counting on 10 by pointing to the 4, so their count ends at 23.

T: Can you put your counter on number five for me?

(Child places a counter on number 5 on their 100-square.)

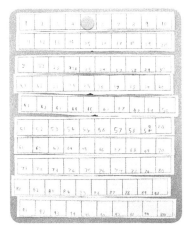

T: I'd like you to tell me, what's ten more than five?

C: *Six!*

T: Is six ten more than five?

C: *Four?*

T: Shall we work it out together? I've got my hundred-square here too. Let's both leave our counter on five. Now shall we use our fingers and count together?

C: *One, two, three, four, five, six, seven, eight, nine, ten.*

(Child skips some of the numbers on the grid with their finger as they count, ending up on 17.)

T: Ooh, careful, let's use our fingers to move one square at a time. Let's try again together.

C: *One, two, three, four, five, six, seven, eight, nine, ten.*

(Child and teacher touch each square as they count.)

When it is clear that a child is simply guessing, how can you help them to build gradually from their existing knowledge?

Directly modelling what actions to make means the child is not having to guess what the teacher wants.

T: So what number is that?

C: *Eleven?*

T: Can you check?

C: *Twelve?*

T: OK. Let's take another look. Let's go back to our counter on number five. Do you remember how many we need to add on?

C: *Ten?*

T: Right. So why don't I keep a track of the ten that we need to count on, on my fingers, and you say the numbers for me.

C: *Six, seven, eight, nine, ten, eleven, twelve, thirteen, fourteen, fifteen.*

(Teacher keeps track on her fingers and prompts child to stop by showing that she has put out ten fingers.)

C: *Fifteen?*

T: It's fifteen. Well done.

> Sharing the task helps the child focus on the number sequence.

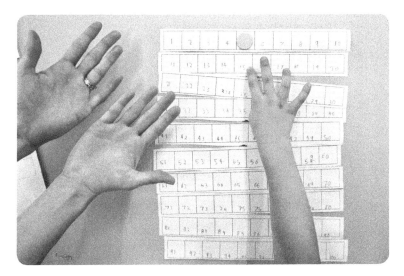

What next?

Work with children to make 2-digit numbers with 10-frames and counters and find the matching numeral on a 100-square.

Going deeper

Ask children to circle a number on a 100-square and to count on in fives. What patterns can they find?

Example 1

T: Can you circle the number forty-three?

(Child circles number 43 on their 100-square.)

T: Can you tell me, what is five more than forty-three?

C: *Five more than forty-three is forty-eight.*

T: Right, so circle forty-eight.

(Child does so.)

T: And five more than forty-eight?

C: *Fifty-two.*

T: Are you sure?

(Child checks by counting on from 48.)

C: *Fifty-three.*

(Child circles 53.)

T: Five more than fifty-three?

C: *Fifty-eight.*

(Child circles fifty-eight.)

T: And five more than fifty-eight?

C: *Sixty-three.*

T: Have you noticed a pattern?

C: *So you start here, then you go to here, then you go to this and you land on the same number.*

(Child points to numbers in the two columns – numerals ending in 3 and 5.)

T: Always the same number?

C: *No, two different numbers.*

T: OK, what bit of the number is the same?

C: *The three and the eight.*

T: Good, so what part of the number is that?

C: *The ones?*

T: Good, the ones digit is always three, eight, three, eight.

> Can children say the number that is five more than their number without having to count on in ones?

▲ Five more than fifty-eight is sixty-three.

> How can you probe children's thinking, without leading them too much?

Example 2

T: Good, let's do another one. Can you put your counter on the number four for me, and can you tell me what twenty more than four would be?

C: *Twenty-four.*

T: And what would twenty more than twenty-four be?

C: *Forty-four.*

T: And twenty more?

C: *Sixty-four.*

T: And twenty more than that?

C: *Eighty-four.*

T: And twenty more than that?

C: *A hundred and four.*

T: Good!

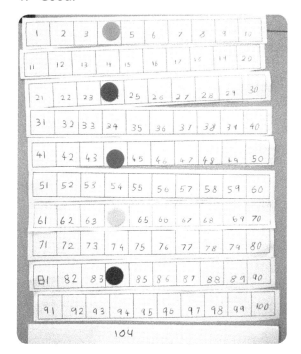

How might asking a child how they answered so quickly deepen their understanding?

For children who are skip counting reliably to numbers up to 100, are they confident in crossing the 100 boundary?

What next?

Children predict the patterns for beyond 100. How can they check if they are right? They also explore the patterns when counting on in fours.

Tasks in Practice

Learning task 4: Take five blocks

(DP) Year 1 > Term 3 > Unit 14 > Number and place value >
Week 1 > Learning task 4

**In this task, children make and put in order as many
different numbers as they can, using exactly five pieces of
base-ten apparatus.**

On track

Children who are 'on track' explain why 50 is the largest
number possible with five blocks (using five 10-rods) and 5 is
the smallest (using five 1-cubes) and find the position of the
number on a number line.

T: OK, two questions for you. What's the smallest number you
can make with the rods and cubes? And what's the largest
number you can make? And why?

C1: *Five.*

T: Five what?

C1: *Five little cubes. It's the smallest number.*

T: Why is that the smallest number?

C1: *Because five ones.*

T: Show me with the equipment.

(Child puts five 1-cubes in the ones column of
their place value frame.)

T: What does everyone else think? Has
anybody got an idea to match that, or that
is different?

C2: *Zero?*

T: How can you make zero if you have to have
five pieces of equipment?

C2: *Oh yes! Then I think the smallest number is
five ones.*

> When a child is answering
> confidently, why might we
> still want them to show the
> answer practically?

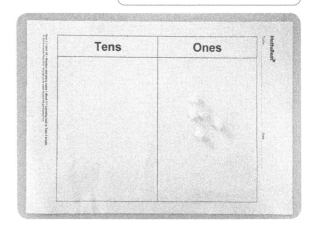

▲ Five is the smallest number you can make with five
pieces of base-ten apparatus.

T: Why do you think that?

C2: *Because you have five pieces, but a ten would make it larger.*

T: What would happen if you changed a one to a ten?

C2: *It would be bigger.*

T: It would make the number larger, wouldn't it?

C2: *Yes. The largest number is fifty.*

T: Why is that?

C2: *Because it's five tens and five pieces of equipment so it's fifty.*

> Mathematical vocabulary is developed by helping children express themselves more accurately.

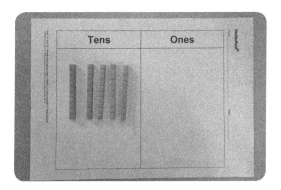

▲ Fifty is the largest number you can make.

T: So five tens is the largest, because you can only have five pieces of equipment. And tens are bigger than ones. Is he right?

C3: *Yes. I think the largest number is fifty and the smallest number is five.*

T: So you agree. Good.

> *Can you explain why you agree? Could you show me with your equipment?*

What next?

Ask children how many different numbers they can make with five blocks, and how they will know they have found all the combinations. Look for children who can explain that there are six combinations and that if they start with five ones, they can replace a one with a ten each time until they have five tens. Children investigate what numbers can be made using eight blocks.

Needing support

Look and listen for children who, having selected their number using base-ten apparatus, mark the number on the number line too far away from a reasonable estimate.

This child has selected one 10-rod and four 1-cubes.

T: Put the ten on your place value frame.

(Child moves a 1-cube into the tens column.)

T: The green one is worth ten.

(Teacher places 10-rod in tens column.)

T: Right, let's add on. We've got ten ...

C: *Nine ...*

T: Eleven ...

C: *Twelve, thirteen, fourteen.*

(Teacher moves each 1-cube into the ones column.)

T: Can you see where fourteen might go on your number line?

C: *I think it would go here?*

(Child points to 40.)

T: Hmm is that fourteen? Where's ten on your number line?

C: *Here.*

T: Okay, so add on just four more. If this is ten and this is twenty, would we get to twenty if we added on four?

C: *No.*

T: No, so where would we get to?

C: *Here, or here, or here, or here.*

(Child points at multiples of 10 up to 40.)

T: You're jumping in tens. We need to count in ones. Can you find ten on a metre stick?

(Child counts along to 10 on the metre stick.)

T: Now let's add on four more. So find ten and add on four more.

C: *One, two, three, four ...*

(Child goes to keep counting.)

T: And then we stop, don't we? What number have we landed on?

C: *Fourteen.*

> How could the child be supported to correctly position this apparatus on the place value frame?

> *Look again at that number. Can you tell me what it is? How many tens and how many ones?*

Needing support

Look and listen for children who find it difficult to hold onto the parameters of the problem (only five pieces allowed).

T: What was the largest number?

C: *Fifty-five.*

T: Can you show me?

(Child shows five 10-rods and five 1-cubes.)

T: How many pieces of equipment are you allowed to use?

C: *Five.*

T: How many have you used?

C: *Five tens and five ones. So ten.*

T: Ah. So, what's the largest number you can make only using five pieces?

C: *Five of those* (child points to the 10-rods). *No, four of those and one to make fifty-one.*

T: How many have you got there?

C: *Five.*

T: We have five pieces of equipment. What is the value? Count in tens.

C: *Ten, twenty, thirty, forty, and then fifty-one.*

T: Fifty-one?

C: *No, forty-one.*

T: Is that the most you can have? How much is this worth?

(Teacher points to the 1-cube.)

C: *One.*

T: Could we swap it for something that's worth more?

C: *Yes. Another ten? Ten, twenty, thirty, forty, fifty.*

T: Is fifty worth more than forty-one?

C: *Yes.*

▲ Check children are using the right amount of equipment.

> *How much more is it worth? Can you show me?*

What next?

Children record the different numbers they can make with five blocks, each on a separate slip of paper, and then put them in order.

Going deeper

We are going to change the rules a little! You must still use five pieces of base-ten apparatus, but now you can choose from 1-cubes, 10-rods and 100-flats. What is the smallest number you can make? What is the largest?

T: We're going to introduce hundreds now. If you could have five of these (teacher holds up a 1-cube), **five of these** (teacher holds up a 10-rod), **or five of these** (teacher holds up a 100-flat), **or a mixture, but still only five pieces, what would be the largest number you could make?**

C: *Ten. No? Fifty? No, one hundred and fifty?*

T: Get your whiteboards and pens out. You can draw a square for a hundred, a line for a ten and a dot for a one. Ok, so I can only have five pieces of apparatus. What combination could I have to make the smallest, and the largest number?

C: *All one hundreds.*

T: How many?

C: *Five.*

T: OK, so one, two, three, four, five hundreds.

(Teacher draws five squares.)

T: We've got five one-hundreds. What's that altogether?

C: *Five hundred.*

> How could you check children's understanding of the value of each piece of equipment before starting the problem?

> The teacher takes care to clarify what 'five' is referring to.

▲ Five-hundred is the largest number you can make.

T: Why did you choose that one?

C: *Because it's the highest out of all of them.*

T: Yes, it's going to be the largest number. So if you've got five of the largest you're going to have what?

C: *Five hundred.*

T: Well done. So what's the smallest number you can make?

C: *One.*

T: But if I use one, am I following the rule? What is the rule?

C: *Oh, I need five. It's five then.*

T: How do you know five is the smallest number you can make?

C: *Because the one-cube is the smallest number, so if we use five of them that must be less than if we use any of these ones.*

T: Well done.

> Can you predict what would happen if we had to work with six of each?

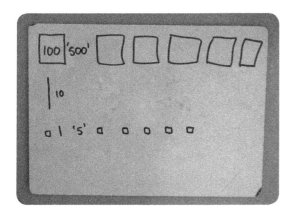

▲ Five-hundred is the largest number and five is the smallest number you can make.

What next?

This time, you must still use five pieces of base-ten apparatus, but you must include at least one 1-cube, one 10-rod and one 100-flat. What numbers can you make now?

Chapter 2
Addition and subtraction

Strand overview

Aims

Children solve, practically, different problem types – change, collection and comparison. They reason about how such problems involve part-part-whole relationships. They develop fluency in knowing number bonds to 10 and begin to extend this to bonds to 20.

Key ideas

- There are three 'core' experiences underpinning all addition and subtractions problems: change increase (e.g. I had 3 pegs; you gave me 2 more; how many do I have?)/change decrease (e.g. I had 9 pegs; I gave 4 to you; how many do I have?), collection (e.g. I have 4 red pegs and 2 blue pegs; how many altogether?) and comparison (e.g. I have 7 pegs; you have 5; how many more do I have?).

- Children develop a more secure understanding of addition and subtraction by working on both concepts together and talking about part-part-whole relationships.

- Many subtraction problems can be solved by addition (I have 14 cherries and eat 12, how many do I have left? 12 plus 2 is 14). Making explicit the part-part-whole relationship in a problem helps children reason about different ways to do the calculation.

- Children will need time to understand that some subtraction problems can be solved using addition.

- Children need to relate numbers to 5 and 10 to become confident with number bonds to 20, e.g. given 8 + 7, thinking of 7 as 2 + 5.

- Becoming fluent in number bonds builds on using strategies such as '5 and a bit' (8 + 7 = 5 + 3 + 5 + 2 = 10 + 3 + 2), bridging to 10 (8 + 7 = 8 + 2 + 5) and near doubles (8 + 7 = double 8 subtract 1).

Models and apparatus

Concrete apparatus such as cubes, bead strings, number rods and 10-frames help to reveal the structure of part-part-whole relationships. Children represent these pictorially, by drawing part-part-whole and bar models. They use 0–20 number lines to model their strategies.

 View the video on the Year 1 Teacher Support area of the Digital Planner

Progression through the National Curriculum

EYFS

- Automatically recall number bonds for numbers 0–5 and for 10, including corresponding partitioning facts.

- Automatically recall double facts up to 5 + 5.

Year 1

- Read, write and interpret mathematical statements involving addition (+), subtraction (–) and equals (=) signs.

- Represent and use number bonds and related subtraction facts within 20.

- Add and subtract 1-digit and 2-digit numbers to 20, including zero.

- Solve one-step problems that involve addition and subtraction, using concrete objects and pictorial representations, and missing number problems such as 7 = ☐ – 9.

Year 2

- Solve problems with addition and subtraction:

  ◦ using concrete objects and pictorial representations, including those involving numbers, quantities and measures

  ◦ applying their increasing knowledge of mental and written methods.

- Recall and use addition and subtraction facts to 20 fluently, and derive and use related facts up to 100.

- Add and subtract numbers using concrete objects, pictorial representations, and mentally, including:

  ◦ a 2-digit number and ones

  ◦ a 2-digit number and tens

  ◦ two 2-digit numbers

  ◦ adding three 1-digit numbers.

- Show that addition of two numbers can be done in any order (commutative) and subtraction of one number from another cannot.

- Recognize and use the inverse relationship between addition and subtraction and use this to check calculations and solve missing number problems.

Year 1 sub-objectives

Term 1

- Read, write and interpret mathematical statements involving addition (+) and equals (=) signs.
- Read, write and interpret mathematical statements involving subtraction (–) and equals (=) signs.
- Represent and use number bonds within 10.
- Represent and use subtraction facts within 10.
- Add 1-digit numbers to 10.
- Subtract 1-digit numbers to 10.
- Solve one-step problems that involve addition, using concrete objects and pictorial representations and numbers to 10.
- Solve one-step problems that involve subtraction, using concrete objects and pictorial representations and numbers to 10.

Term 2

- Read, write and interpret mathematical statements involving addition (+), subtraction (–) and equals (=) signs.
- Represent and use number bonds within 10.
- Represent and use subtraction facts within 10.
- Represent and use number bonds within 20.
- Represent and use subtraction facts within 20.
- Add and subtract 1-digit and 2-digit numbers to 20.
- Solve one-step problems that involve addition and subtraction, using concrete objects and pictorial representations and numbers to 20.
- Solve missing number problems such as $7 = \square - 9$ (within 20).

Term 3

- Read, write and interpret mathematical statements involving addition (+), subtraction (–) and equals (=) signs.
- Represent and use number bonds within 20.
- Represent and use subtraction facts within 20.
- Add and subtract 1-digit and 2-digit numbers to 20.
- Add and subtract 1-digit and 2-digit numbers to 20, including zero.
- Solve one-step problems that involve addition and subtraction, using concrete objects and pictorial representations and numbers to 20.
- Solve missing number problems such as $7 = \square - 9$ (within 20).

Tasks in practice

Learning task 1: How many dinosaurs in the cave?

DP Year 1 > Term 1 > Unit 4 > Addition and subtraction > Week 9 > Learning task 1

In this task, children explore part-part-whole relationships.

On track

Children who are 'on track' use objects to calculate missing quantities.

5 dinosaurs are on the table, and 1 is hidden under a piece of tissue paper to represent a 'cave'.

T: How many dinosaurs did you have altogether?

C: *Six.*

T: Our whole number is six. How many are outside the cave?

C: *One, two, three, four, five.*

(Child counts the dinosaurs.)

T: So how many are inside the cave?

C: *One.*

T: Why do you think one?

C: *Because you got one in there and five out there.*

T: What would one and five make?

C: *Six.*

T: Shall we check?

(Child lifts up the tissue to confirm their answer.)

T: Can you write the addition sentence? What are we going to start with?

C: *Six.*

T: That's our whole number, isn't it?

C: *One add five equals six.*

T: Well done.

> Using a 10-frame to represent the problem, could encourage children to calculate without counting in ones.

> If a child suggests starting with the whole (6) a different number sentence could be discussed and recorded, e.g. 6 equals 1 add 5. All the following number sentences could be recorded to match this one.

On track

Children who are 'on track' describe part changes for the same whole, e.g. If we add one to one of the parts, the other part will be one fewer.

Children have explored several ways to partition 6 dinosaurs.

T: Did the whole number change, or did the parts change?

C: *The parts changed.*

T: You had four and two. What were another two parts that you had?

C: *Three and three. Two and four.*

T: Very good. What is the smallest number of dinosaurs that could come out of the cave?

C: *Zero.*

T: How many would be inside the cave?

C: *Six.*

T: How could I write that as an addition sentence?

C: *Zero add six equals six.*

T: Very good. You have added two parts to make the whole. If it was zero this time, what could come out next time?

C: *One.*

T: How many would be inside now?

C: *Five.*

T: How would I write this number sentence?

C: *One add five equals six.*

(Child continues to alter the parts up to 0 dinosaurs inside the cave and 6 outside the cave.)

> If a child appears to have spotted a pattern, you could use a bead string to support the emerging understanding of the relationships they are noticing.

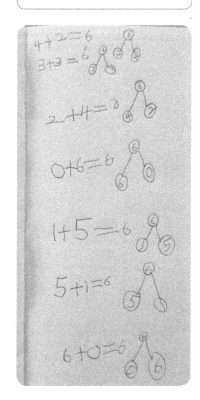

What next?

Children play the game again and record the stories using subtraction sentence frames, e.g. 6 subtract 2 equals 4.

▲ The child has recorded all of the part-part-whole relationships. Could they organize these to show the pattern of one part increasing while the other decreases?

Needing support

Look and listen for children who need support to work out hidden quantities, and those who need support to describe part changes for the same whole.

T: So we started with six dinosaurs in the cave, and two dinosaurs went outside. Now we need to do the number fact. Can you draw the part-part-whole model in your book?

(Child draws the model, but hesitates before writing any numbers.)

T: How many dinosaurs do we have altogether? Can you remember?

C: *Five. And then one. So, seven.*

T: Let's use the dinosaurs to check that.

(Child counts the dinosaurs.)

C: *Six.*

T: So, we write six in the big circle. How many are outside?

C: *Two.*

T: Do you want to write that in your part-part-whole model?

(Child writes 2 in one part.)

T: OK. If there are two outside, how many do you think are inside?

C: *I think four.*

T: OK. Why do you think four? Let's use these.

(Teacher gives child 6 cubes.)

C: *Well, six here and there are two outside. So, move two away?*

(Child takes away 2 cubes.) *So, there are four left.*

T: Well done. So what number should go in here?

(Teacher points to the second part in the model.)

C: *Four.*

T: Good.

> Having a 10-frame and double-sided counters available for the child to refer to during this task will support them to see the number relationships more clearly.

> Does the child understand that 2 is a part here? Are they placing the 2 in the part because there is already 6 in the whole?

> How could you check the child understands and is not simply repeating the number four again?

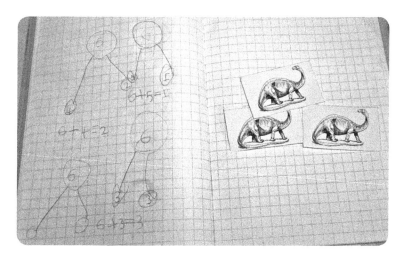

▲ Look at your number sentence again. Which are the parts (the dinosaurs inside and outside the cave) and which is the whole (the total number of dinosaurs)?

What next?
Children work through all the combinations to 6 independently. Support children in expressing this clearly using part-part-whole models and/or number sentences if needed.

Going deeper

Ask children how many different possibilities there would be for 10 dinosaurs.

This child has chosen to find all the possible combinations for 10 dinosaurs, and write the matching addition and subtraction number sentences.

T: I've hidden some of the dinosaurs in the cave. How many have come out?

C: *Four.*

T: So how many are in the cave?

C: *Six.*

T: How do you know?

C: *There are four outside the cave, so there must be six in there. Because that makes ten.*

T: I see! So, did you use a fact you already know to help you?

C: *Yes. I know that six and four makes ten.*

T: Can you show me on your paper?

(Child records in a part-part-whole model.)

T: Lovely, now can you make a number sentence?

C: *Six add four equals ten.*

T: Can you think of any more?

C: *Ten take away four equals six.*

T: Lovely. Is there another way?

C: *Ten take away six equals four.*

T: Is there another addition sentence you can make? You added this part to this part to make the whole. Is there a different way you could do it?

C: *Four add six.*

> *You are finding all fact families for the number ten. How many do you think there will be?*

> How do you encourage children to verbalize their thinking?

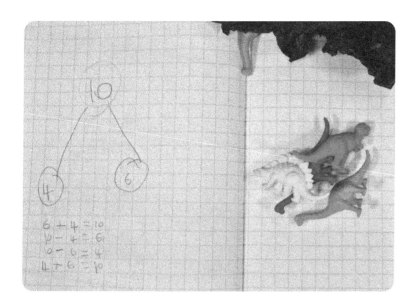

T: What can you tell me about your two additions?

C: *The parts are the same. But I've changed the order. It's still ten.*

T: Well done.

C: I'm going to make one more dinosaur come out of the cave. So, then it is five outside. So there must be five inside. Five and five is ten.

(Child goes on to find all of the combinations to 10 and puts them in order.)

What if there were nine dinosaurs instead of ten? How would that change the number sentences you have made? Is there more than one way?

What next?

Do you think there will be more or fewer combinations for 9 than there were for 10? Prove it.

Tasks in Practice

Learning task 2: Fewer on the bus

(DP) Year 1 > Term 2 > Unit 9 > Addition and subtraction >
Week 3 > Learning task 2

In this task, children play a subtraction game involving subtracting 10 from numbers 10–20.

On track

Children who are 'on track' use their knowledge of '10 + ones' number facts (e.g. 10 + 7 = 17) to solve 10-fewer problems such as 17 – 10 = 7.

One child has chosen a numeral card at random (17) to decide how many passengers to put on a bus. Another child must take away 10 passengers and say how many are left. The bus-seat plan is represented by two 10-frames.

C: *So I started to do a part-part-whole model, and then I did a bar model.*

T: First of all, can you tell me what's in your 10-frames?

C: *This is one full 10-frame.*

T: And how many is in that?

C: *Ten.*

T: And what's in the other 10-frame?

C: *Seven.*

T: So if ten people get off the bus, what do you do with the 10-frames?

C: *You take away ten passengers and that leaves you with seven. Because if you get seven plus ten that equals seventeen and take away ten that equals seven.*

> What is the advantage of using 10-frames at this point in the task?

> What does this child's statement tell us about their understanding of the relationship between addition and subtraction? What is supporting this understanding?

T: Very good. So why do you start with this 10-frame when you want to take them away? (Teacher points to the full 10-frame).

C: *It's easier. Because I can take away ten all at once.*

What other models and images might support this emerging understanding? Bead strings? 100-squares? How are these the same and how are they different?

T: Great. So what can you tell me about your part-part-whole model?

C: *So the whole is the one that is in the middle, that's seventeen, and the parts are the ones that have the lines going to them. I need to write ten and seven as the parts.*

T: Very good, and what about your bar model, what numbers have you got in there?

C: *I've got seventeen, ten and seven.*

T: Very good, well done.

So what is the same in your 10-frames, your part-part-whole model and your bar model?

What next?
Children set up similar bus problems for their partners to solve.

Needing support

Look and listen for children who count in ones to solve 10-fewer problems.

T: There are nineteen people on the bus. Can you do that in cubes on the 10-frames?

(Child starts counting out cubes one at a time into the right-hand 10-frame. He puts cubes 11 and 12 below the 10-frame.)

> As a prerequisite to this task, children can play games where they fill 10-frames until no more can fit, e.g. roll a dice, put that number of cubes into a 10-frame, first person to fill a complete 10-frame wins. Extend to filling two 10-frames.

T: How many have we got so far?

C: *One, two, three, four, five, six, seven, eight, nine, ten, eleven, twelve.*

T: We need to start using the other 10-frame! Let's move these.

(Teacher moves the extra 2 cubes into the second 10-frame.)

T: We've got twelve. We need nineteen. Let's keep going.

C: *One, two, three, four, five, six, seven, eight …*

(Child fills the rest of the second 10-frame.)

T: Let's stop here for a second because that's two full 10-frames. How many cubes have we got?

C: *I'll take some away?*

(Child removes 2 cubes.)

> Labelling how many we have so far can help children to count on rather than start the count sequence again, e.g. How many do we have? 12. Let's make a label on this square to remind us. So now let's add one more – 13, good. 14, 15 …

T: Remember we're trying to get to nineteen. How many have we got now?

(Child counts up in ones.)

C: *Eighteen.*

T: How many more do we need?

(Child adds another cube.)

C: *I've got nineteen now.*

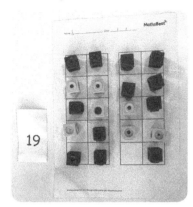

T: Great. Now we need to take ten away. Will you help me count ten off? Let's start here.

(Teacher starts on the 10-frame that is not full.)

C: *One, two, three, four, five, six, seven, eight, nine, ten.*

T: How many have we got left?

C: *One, two, three, four, five, six, seven, eight, nine.*

> How could you support a child to stop relying on counting in ones? What strategies do you use to move children on from this?

What next?

Give children a set of flash cards for the numbers 10–20 with each number represented on two 10-frames, one full and the other partially full. Ask the child to cover one whole 10 on a card and say how many are left. Can you see 10 in the picture? How many are there if the 10-frame is full? Is there a really easy way to cover one whole 10 on the picture?

Going deeper

Ask children to make up 'how many were there' problems based on their cards to challenge other pairs to solve, e.g. 7 are left, 10 got off. How many were on the bus?

This child has been set a problem with an unknown start:
? – 10 = 4.

T: Your partner has made up this problem for you: 'At the first stop there were a certain amount of passengers who got on. At the second stop, ten passengers got off. Then there were four passengers left. How many did we start with?' That's a nice problem. What answer did you get?

C: *Fourteen.*

T: Fourteen. I can see you've already shown that on a part-part-whole model. Can you show it on a bar model?

(Child starts drawing a bar model.)

T: You had fourteen to begin with, so that's the whole. What are the two parts?

C: *Ten and four.*

> How do you support children with working backwards to solve problems where the start is unknown?

(Child writes 14, 10 and 4 in the bar model.)

T: Ten and four, very good! Can you tell me the story about this bar model?

C: *Fourteen children were on the bus. By the next stop four children were left on the bus.*

T: Can you show me with cubes what happened in the story?

C: *There were fourteen children on the bus, then ten got off and then there were four left.*

(Child demonstrates with cubes on two 10-frames.)

T: We know that there were four children left at the end and ten children had already got off, so what did you do to find out the original number on the bus? What is the opposite of subtraction?

C: *Adding.*

T: So, how many did you add to four to find out the whole?

C: *Ten.*

T: Ten, very good.

> What is the value of asking the child to tell the story in this way? How is it supporting their mathematical thinking?

> How could this problem be represented as an addition number sentence? Could it be represented with a subtraction number sentence? Where would the empty boxes be in each of these?

What next?

Give children the numbers 10, 8 and 18. Ask them to make three different problems that each use these numbers only once. Their answers should be 8, 10 and 18, e.g. 10 + 8 = 18.

Tasks in Practice

Learning task 3: Add it then take it away

(DP) Year 1 > Term 3 > Unit 15 > Addition and subtraction > Week 2 > Learning task 3

In this task, children add on a number then subtract it on a partially labelled number line, to convince themselves of the inverse relationship between addition and subtraction.

On track

Children who are 'on track' show you that when you add a number and then subtract it again you get back to the number you started with.

Children have blue cards numbered 7–14, and white cards numbered 4–6. Children select a blue card and a white card at random. They use a number line to add the white number to the blue number. They then use a number line to subtract the white number from the answer.

T: Do you notice any patterns in this pair of equations?

(Teacher points to where a child has written 12 + 4 = 16 and 16 – 4 = 12.)

C: *They both have a sixteen.*

T: Anything else?

C: The number that we jump stays the same: four and four, and six and six.

(Child points to their earlier working: 14 + 6 = 20 and 20 – 6 = 14.)

T: Well spotted. What else can we see?

C: They start with twelve?

T: Can you show me on here?

C: So we start with twelve, we do the four jumps, we land on sixteen.

(Child shows how they modelled 12 + 4 = 16 on a number line.)

T: And what about this calculation?

(Teacher points to 16 – 4 = 12.)

C: We go back four and we get to twelve.

T: Good. We get back to the same part. If you have a start number, and you add something then take it away, do you think you always get back to your start number?

C: Yes.

T: Why do you think that?

C: Because if you were on twelve and then you go to sixteen, then if you go back the same amount of jumps you get back to twelve. Four jumps, so if you went back four jumps you'll always land on twelve.

T: So you think if the number of jumps stays the same you'll always get back to your start number?

C: Yes, it's like you add and take away the same, so you are back to where you started.

> Here the child is beginning to generalize by referring to more than one example and comparing them. What supports children to make this kind of connection?

> How do you use paired work to refine children's explanations?

> *What if we started at twelve, added six then took away three twice? Can you explain what happens this time?*

What next?

Children explore their hypothesis with the examples they've recorded and then test again using their own choice of number. If children are making jumps in ones on the number line, encourage them to make bigger jumps, using their number facts for 10 to support them.

Needing support

Look and listen for children who find it difficult to see the number they started with, and those who see each calculation separately rather than looking for the similarities between each example.

This child has selected blue card 14 for their start number and white card 5 to add on.

T: We're adding first. If we're adding, are we going forwards or backwards on our number line?

C: Forwards.

T: Good. Which number are we starting from?

C: Fourteen.

(Child counts and records the 5 jumps.)

T: Circle that number you landed on. What number is that?

C: Nine. No, nineteen.

T: Can you write the equation? What number did you start on?

C: Fourteen.

T: How much are we adding? How many jumps did we do?

C: Five.

(Child writes 14 + 5.)

T: What number did you land on?

(Child re-counts the 5 jumps from 14.)

C: Nineteen.

T: So what are we going to write?

(Child writes = 19.)

T: Well done. Now we'll subtract. For adding, we went forwards. Which way shall we go for subtracting?

C: Backwards.

T: Lovely. Let's write it. What's the number you started with?

C: Nineteen.

(Child counts back 5 and lands on 14.)

> What would be the advantages of asking this child to count on one to 15 and then explore other ways to add on the remaining 4?

> The child needs to re-count at this point because they have a lot to focus on here. Creating the number sentences with number and symbol cards alongside the number line might help to reduce this.

T: Let's check with cubes. We are going to subtract, what do you need to do?

C: *Take away five.*

(Child counts 5 cubes out from the 19.)

T: We had nineteen.

(Teacher writes 19 – ☐.)

T: How much did you subtract?

C: *Five.*

T: Well remembered. Write five for me.

(Child writes 5.)

T: Is equal to ...? How many do you have left?

(Child counts remaining cubes one by one.)

T: So what would the answer be?

(Child writes 14.)

T: Good. Do both equations have all the same numbers?

C: *Yes.*

T: So what's different? One is ...?

(Teacher points to the addition symbol.)

C: *Add.*

T: Add. And one is ...?

C: *Subtract.*

T: Exactly!

> How could the interlocking cubes be structured to avoid the need to re-count all of them? Could colour blocking into 14 red and 5 blue help, for example?

▲ Show me the fourteen cubes. Where is the fourteen in each equation? Show me the five cubes. And in the equations? Where are the nineteen cubes in each equation? What is staying the same? What is changing?

What next?

Children work through a series of examples where only one is added each time, e.g. start with 2, add 1 then take away 1; start with 3, add 1 then take away 1; start with 4 ... Children create the first example with cubes, then change the cubes to show the second example. What has stayed the same? What has changed?

Going deeper

Ask children to record their calculations on number lines with 0, 5, 10, 15 and 20 marked but no intermediate tick marks.

This child writes 8 + 5 = 13.

T: Can you check your answer on the number line?

C: *Yes, I know that eight add two equals ten, so I'll do that jump first. Then I could add the other three. That would be five altogether.*

(Child records the position of 8 on the line by counting forward approximately 3 from the 5 that is marked, draws a jump from 8 to 10 on top of the number line and writes '+ 2'. Child then draws a jump from 10 to 13 and writes '+ 3' on top and '13' underneath the line).

C: *Now I'm at thirteen.*

T: OK. Now I'd like you to take away one more than you added. So, what number are you going to take away?

C: *Six, because it's one more than five.*

T: Good, six. Which number are you going to take six away from?

C: *Thirteen.*

(On the number line, child draws a jump back 3 to 10 and writes '– 3', then another jump of 3 to 7 and writes '– 3' and '7' under the line)

C: *Seven.*

(Child records 13 – 6 = 7.)

> Fluency in the bonds of 10 supports this strategic approach.

> *Can you explain how you did this without counting back in ones?*

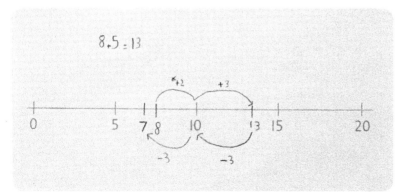

T: What do you notice about your two equations?

C: *Both have thirteen, but seven is one less than eight, and six is one more than five.*

T: The number you take away is always one more than the number you added. So will the number you get back to always be one less than your start number?

> How could the child be supported to describe the rule?

C: *I think so?*

T: Let's do another example.

(Teacher writes 11 + 6 = 17.)

T: Then we do seventeen take away one more than six. What's one more than six?

C: *Seven.*

(Teacher writes 17 – 7 = ☐.)

T: If you know that eleven add six is seventeen, and we're doing seventeen take away one more than six, what do you think the answer will be?

C: *Eighteen.*

T: Why do you think it's eighteen?

C: *Because it's one more than seventeen.*

T: What would seventeen take away six be?

C: *Eleven.*

(Child writes 17 – 6 = 11.)

T: If I took away one more than six what do you think the answer would be?

> What could help the child realize that the language of 'more than' here is actually subtracting?

C: *Twelve?*

T: Shall we check on your number line?

(Child jumps back 7 from 17 to 10 and writes '– 7'.)

C: *Oh, it's ten!*

T: Yes, well done. What do you notice?

C: *Ten is one less than eleven and seven is one more than six.*

> Does this fit with our rule? How can we test it out further?

What next?

Children test out the pattern together. They predict what the answers will be, before checking on the number line.

Chapter 3
Multiplication and division

Strand overview

Aims

Children solve, practically, multiplication problems involving the core idea of creating equal groups. They solve, practically, division problems that involve grouping or equal sharing. They reason, in practical and visual situations, about multiplication being commutative. By finding the total number of items in simple arrays, they begin to become fluent in skip counting and reason how this can be quicker than counting in ones.

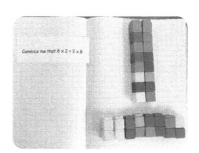

Key ideas

• A big step from addition to multiplication is the idea of 'unitizing': moving from using 'one' to represent a single object (e.g. one finger) to 'one' representing 'one group' (e.g. one hand has five fingers). It takes time for children to develop this understanding.

• Most multiplication problems are very simple rate problems (e.g. There are five plates on a table and three biscuits on each plate – this is a 1 (plate) to 3 (biscuits) rate). The word 'each' in a problem flags that it is simple rate.

• Solving division problems with equal sharing (e.g. 3 friends share 9 biscuits equally; how many does each get?) and solving division problems with grouping (e.g. There are 15 plums; a punnet holds 5 plums; how many punnets can be filled?) involve different actions and children need plenty of experience of each.

• Exploring arrays, and talking about different ways to describe them and find the total (e.g. a 2 by 5 array can be seen as 2 equal groups of 5 or 5 equal groups of 2) provides an informal introduction to the idea that multiplication is commutative.

Models and apparatus

Literal representations of problems can help reveal the structure and the context, e.g. real fruit to share between plates, or physical arrays such as egg trays. Children then move on to using objects such as cubes to represent the real items. To help children relate to multiplication problems, draw on naturally occurring equal groups, e.g. 2 eyes per face; 5 fingers per hand; 10 toes per person.

 View the video on the Year 1 Teacher Support area of the Digital Planner

Progression through the National Curriculum

EYFS

- Automatically recall double facts up to 5 + 5.
- Explore patterns of numbers within numbers up to 10, including evens and odds.

Year 1

- Solve one-step problems involving multiplication and division, by calculating the answer using concrete objects, pictorial representations and arrays with the support of the teacher.

Year 2

- Recall and use multiplication and division facts for the 2, 5 and 10 multiplication tables, including recognizing odd and even numbers.

- Calculate mathematical statements for multiplication and division within the multiplication tables and write them using the multiplication (×), division (÷) and equals (=) signs.

- Show that multiplication of two numbers can be done in any order (commutative) and division of one number by another cannot.

- Solve problems involving multiplication and division, using materials, arrays, repeated addition, mental methods, and multiplication and division facts, including problems in contexts.

Year 1 sub-objectives

Term 1

- Solve one-step problems involving multiplication, by calculating the answer using concrete objects.
- Solve one-step problems involving division, by calculating the answer using concrete objects.

Term 2

- Solve one-step problems involving multiplication, by calculating the answer using concrete objects, pictorial representations and arrays with the support of the teacher.
- Solve one-step problems involving division, by calculating the answer using concrete objects, pictorial representations and arrays with the support of the teacher.

Term 3

- Solve one-step problems involving multiplication, by calculating the answer using concrete objects, pictorial representations and arrays with the support of the teacher.

Tasks in Practice

Learning task 2: What is the same?

DP Year 1 > Term 1 > Unit 6 > Multiplication and division > Week 12 > Learning task 2

In this task, children solve two equal-groups problems that are mathematically equivalent and talk about what is the same and what is different.

On track

Children who are 'on track' talk about the similarities in the problems by making reference to the relationships of the quantities being the same in each, and use the language of 'each' or 'equal' appropriately.

Children are shown this problem and asked to represent it visually:

- Some children are going on a trip.
  There are 2 children in each car.
  There are 4 cars going on the trip.
  How many children altogether go on the trip?

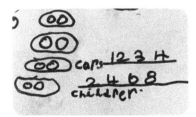

T: Can you see any pattern?

C: *Two, four, six, eight.*

T: Good thinking. Anything else anyone noticed?

C: *There is a pattern as it goes one, two, three, four, and two, four, six, eight.*

T: Great thinking. So, the number of cars is going up in ones and what is the number of people going up in?

C: *Twos.*

> A double number line showing the number of cars and the number of people may draw children's attention to the two patterns that develop in parallel to each other, if they do not spot it.

Children are shown this problem:

- Cara is packing bags of apples.
  She packs 4 bags of apples.
  There are 2 apples in each bag.
  How many apples does Cara pack?

T: This time I've got bags and I've got apples. So, in my first bag how many apples have I got?

C: *Two.*

T: When I've got two bags of apples, how many apples have I got?

C1: *Two.*

C2: *Four.*

T: Have a look at the red counters. This is my first bag of apples and this is my second bag of apples. How many apples have I got?

C1: *Four.*

T: When I have three bags of apples how many have I got?

C: *Six.*

T: And when I've got my four bags of apples, how many apples have I got?

C: *Eight.*

T: What do you notice?

C1: *It's the same as the cars.*

C2: *There is a pattern, like the cars. It's the same pattern.*

T: Good!

▲ If I have three bags of apples, how many apples have I got? Yellow counters were used for cars and red counters are being used for apples.

Do the children need support in 'stepping back' from the particular contexts of cars and apples to think about the similarities between the two problems?

What next?

Children use counters or draw pictures to work out how many children there are in six cars and how many apples there are in six bags.

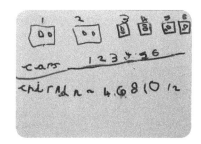

▲ How many children are in 6 cars?

Needing support

Look and listen for children who find it difficult to talk about the problem's underlying mathematical similarities (in other words, they focus on cars and apples, rather than the numbers).

Children are looking at the car problem.

The teacher realizes that some children are struggling with the basics of representing the problem, so gives support in setting up a model with the whole class.

T: There are two children in each car and there are four cars. How many children altogether are going on the trip?

C: *Six.*

T: I think you've added the numbers two and four together. Do you think that is the right thing to do? There are two children in every car and there are four cars. Talk to your partner. What can we do?

C: *We can use our fingers.*

T: What else can we use?

C: *We can use rulers?*

T: How will rulers help us?

C: *We need to find two and add four.*

T: Is that the right way to solve this problem? Are we adding the children and the cars together? Or are we finding out how many children there are altogether?

C: *Finding out how many children there are altogether.*

T: Do you think we might need to act it out? How many cars are there?

C: *Four.*

T: Let's make four cars then.

(Teacher sets out two chairs side by side.)

T: Here is one car. How many people need to get in each car?

C: *Two.*

T: Two people. Can I have two people sitting in this car?

(Two children sit down.)

> A common difficulty where children default to addition as a preferred operation is often uncovered here.

> If children are struggling with the structure of a problem, it is helpful for them to act it out.

T: What do I need to do now?

C: *Get another car.*

(Teacher sets out another pair of chairs and two more children sit down.)

T: Have I got enough cars now?

C: *No, two more cars.*

(Teacher sets out a third pair of chairs. Two more children sit.)

T: Have I got enough cars now?

C: *No, one more.*

T: One more car. A car with three people?

C: *No, two.*

(Teacher sets out a fourth pair of chairs. Two more children sit.)

T: Right, have I got enough cars now?

C: *Yes.*

T: What have we got here then?

C: *Four cars with two people in each car.*

T: How can we find out how many children there are altogether?

C: *Count them. One, two, three, four, five, six, seven, eight.*

T: Eight. Could someone count the children in twos?

C: *Two, four, six, eight.*

T: Well done. When I had one car how many children did I have?

C: *Two.*

T: When I had two cars how many children did I have?

C: *Four.*

(Teacher repeats for three and four cars.)

> As there are two counts going on (cars and children), ensure children are aware which count is being referred to, and that they use clear language when giving explanation, e.g. 2 cars, 4 children.

What next?

Model both problems with counters. Set out the groups of children in one colour and the groups of apples in another. Talk about what is the same and what is different.

Going deeper

Challenge children to make up another problem that would be 'the same' yet different, by changing the context but keeping the numbers and the relationship between them the same.

T: This time you need to make up a problem. The first problem we looked at had two people in each car and four cars. The second problem had two apples in each bag and four bags of apples. Can you make up a problem with groups of two and four lots of the groups? What might you have two of?

C: *Two bananas.*

T: OK. What could the bananas be inside?

C: *Boxes.*

T: Two bananas in each box. There are two bananas in each box, and how many boxes are you going to have?

C: *Four boxes.*

T: Four boxes. Lovely. Why do you think that is the same?

C: *Because the answer is eight.*

T: Yes, the answer is the same, it's eight. Does everyone else agree?

C: *I think it's sort of the same.*

T What do you mean 'sort of'?

C: *Well the answer is eight but it's about different things. But it's still two plus two plus two plus two.*

T: Yes, before we had people in cars, and then apples in bags. Now we have bananas in boxes. But it is still four lots of two.

> How are children learning about the difference between group size and number of groups?

> What impact does seeking this clarification have?

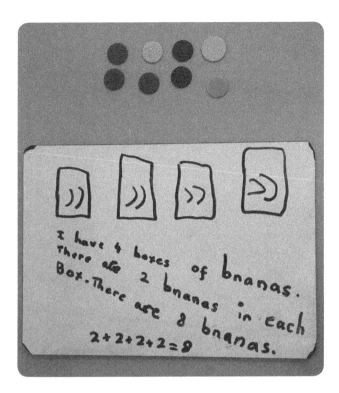

▲ A child's 'banana problem' represented in 4 different ways.

What next?

Give children a problem where the numbers are the same but the relationship is different (e.g. four apples in each of two bags). Can they describe what is the same and what is different?

Tasks in Practice

Learning task 2: What is the same?

 Year 1 > Term 2 > Unit 12 > Multiplication and division >
Week 8 > Learning task 2

In this task, children solve multiplication problems involving arrays, with the context of different flavour muffins.

On track

Children who are 'on track' talk about the similarities in the problems, in terms of the arrays being the same, and explain that it does not matter what flavour the muffins are.

Children are shown the following problems:

1. Sam puts blueberry muffins in rows on a tray.
   Each row has 5 blueberry muffins.
   Sam puts out 2 rows.
   How many blueberry muffins does Sam put out?

2. Sam puts sultana muffins in rows on a tray.
   Sam puts out 2 rows of sultana muffins.
   Each row has 5 sultana muffins.
   How many muffins does Sam put out on the tray?

> What is gained by presenting the problems simultaneously?

The teacher and children have agreed to use counters to represent muffins. They build the array for the first problem together as a class and then work on their tables to build an array for the second problem.

(Child builds an array that is 5 rows of 2.)

T: So, you've got two rows of 5 blueberry muffins that equal ten. And you've created a different array that is five rows of two sultana muffins. Look at the two problems. What do you notice?

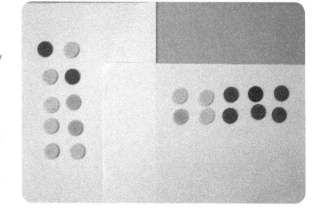

C: *Sultana muffins and blueberry muffins, so they're not the same!*

T: Let's think about the amount of muffins. What's the same?

C: *Ten in both of them.*

T: Great. Let's think about the words in the question. What's the same?

C: *Rows on a tray.*

T: OK, good. Let's look at the second line of the problem: Sam puts out two rows of sultana muffins. And the third line of the first problem said: Sam puts out two rows. What do you notice?

C: *The two is in a different place in each question.*

T: That's interesting isn't it? What else is the same, and what's different?

C: *Each row has five muffins.*

T: Do all your rows have five muffins?

C: *No, I've done two different ways.*

T: Yes, you've done two arrays. Why have you done two arrays?

C: *Because that's another way to make ten.*

T: That's another way to make ten, you're right! Has Sam put his muffins in two different arrays?

C: *No, he has two rows in each and five muffins in each row.*

T: Can you show me?

(Child changes the counters so both arrays show 2 rows of five).

T: What do you notice?

C: *The arrays are the same for blueberry and sultana.*

T: Yes, the muffins are different but the arrays are the same. Good reasoning!

> How is this child directed to think mathematically?

> Asking the child what is the same and what is different will help them to articulate what they notice.

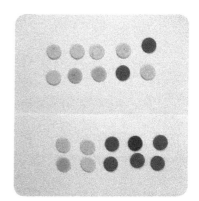

What next?

Children work in pairs and use concrete materials to work out how many rows of muffins Sam could have if baking 12 muffins.

Needing support

Look and listen for children who find it difficult to correctly create the arrays concretely or pictorially.

▲ The child interprets 2 rows of 5 as 2 and 5 and places the digits together to make 25.

This child uses bear counters to represent muffins.

T: You've written 'Sam has 25 sultana muffins'? That's a lot of muffins. Let's have a read of the problem again. Sam puts sultana muffins in rows on a tray. Sam puts out two rows of sultana muffins. Each row has five sultana muffins. OK, each row has five sultana muffins. How many in each row?

C: *Ten.*

T: Hmm … each row has five sultana muffins. How many in each row?

C: *Hmm … Five!*

T: Five. Show me one row of five with your bears.

C: *One, two, three, four, five.*

(Child places bears as they count.)

T: So, this will be a row of five bears. So how could we do another row of five?

C: *Put another five!*

Some children simply place digits they see in a problem together, so 2 rows of 5 becomes 25. How can resources support their sense of operation?

Might counters be more representative of muffins for this problem?

T: Good, so get another row of five out with your bears.

(Child lines up another row of five bears.)

T: So, how are we going to draw this as an array on your tray?

C: *Put bear faces or draw the muffins?*

T: Yes, or we could use circles instead. Show me how you would do it then?

(Child draws two rows of five circles.)

T: Good. So, Sam has twenty-five sultana muffins does he?

C: (Child shakes head.) *Ten!*

T: Good, so change your answer for me.

> *Why might we decide to draw circles instead of bear faces?*

What next?

Set out the array of blueberry muffins in one colour and the array of sultana muffins in another. What is the same and what is different? Children think about a different way of showing 12 muffins. Can they show this with cubes? What is the same and what is different this time?

Going deeper

Ask children to make up a similar type of problem where the total number of muffins is 12. Can they make up more than one problem?

Children have written some word problems. They make arrays using counters to check the numbers they have used in their problems.

C: *One, two, three, four, five, six. Six add six. I'm doing six add six. So, I've got my twelve there.*

(Children count out counters into two rows of six.)

T: Good, so how many rows of muffins do you have? And how many in each row?

C: *Two rows of six.*

T: Good, so how many muffins in total?

C: *Twelve.*

T: Good. Is there another way we could arrange twelve counters into an equal array?

(Child makes two unequal rows.)

T: Is that equal?

C: *No.*

(Child makes 6 rows of 2.)

C: *Now it is equal.*

T: How many rows have we got?

C: *Six.*

T: How many in each row?

C: *Two.*

T: So, we've got six rows with two in each row. Is that an equal array?

C: *Yes.*

T: Well done. So, how is this different to the first array you made?

C: *It's the other way round.*

> Covering up the array, and briefly revealing it may help children subitize the six rather than count in ones.

> *What other language might help reinforce the understanding that arrays have to have equal rows?*

> *How do you know that this array is not equal?*

> *Can you explain how you know that this is an equal array?*

T: Good, so if we turn this array they look the same. So, in one, Sam would have six rows of two muffins, and in the other he would have …

◄ Rotating 2 rows of 6 and 6 rows of 2 to discover commutativity.

C: *Two rows of six muffins.*

T: Excellent. So we have six rows of two muffins and two rows of six muffins. But both times what is the total?

C: *Twelve.*

(Teacher points to another child's array of 4 rows of 3 counters.)

T: What about that array? Chat to each other about what it shows.

What muffin story does it represent?

What next?
Children make up, share and show similar muffin problems with different totals such as 15 and 9.

Tasks in Practice

Learning task 2: Quick glimpses

 Year 1 > Term 3 > Unit 18 > Multiplication and division > Week 7 > Learning task 2

In this task, children try and work out the number in an array without counting in ones.

On track

Children who are 'on track' subitize (recognize the number in a small group without having to count them all) the number of dots in either a row or a column and work with that factor to find the composite number (a number with more than two factors).

The teacher shows an array of 8 counters, in 2 rows of 4.

T: What can you see in this array?

C: *Two fours.*

T: You can see two fours. What do you mean by two fours?

C: *Because there's four up there and a four on the bottom and it's eight.*

T: Good. You can see that there's two rows and that there's four in each row. So we have got two groups of four. And that can also be written as four multiplied by two. So, what does that equal? How many have we got altogether?

> Although we often say 'two times four', the teacher is carefully using the correct mathematical expression.

C: *Eight.*

T: We've got eight altogether.

(Teacher now shows an array of 8 counters, in 4 rows of 2.)

T: OK, so what have we got over here?

C: *Columns.*

T: Good. So, first we had rows and now we have columns. But how many groups have we got?

> The array has changed but notice how the child is still drawn to the 4, which is the number in each column. There are 2 columns of 4.

C: *Two.*

T: Have we got two groups? Are there two rows?

C: *Four.*

T: Yes, we've got four rows. We've got four groups of how many?

C: *Two.*

T: Two, we've got four groups of two. And what does four groups of two equal?

C: *Eight.*

T: Good.

How might a speaking frame have supported the alternative array, e.g.

____ rows of ____

____ groups of ____

What next?

Give groups of children 9 or 12 counters. What arrays could you make with this number of counters? Remind children about equal rows.

▲ Can you make a different array with nine counters?

Needing support

Look and listen for children who find it difficult to recognize one composite unit, either in a row or column. For example, in a 4 by 5 array they find it difficult to tell that there are 4 rows of 5 dots.

The teacher is working with children on arrays to help them 'see' one composite unit.

T: OK, so the array that I would like you to draw is two groups of five. So, what's the first thing you need to do?

C: *Get two.*

T: You could get two, but we need two groups of five. So, what are you going to do?

C: *Get another two.*

T: OK. So what have you got there? You've got: one group of two, two groups of two.

(Child gets another two counters.)

T: What do you have now? Three groups of how many?

C: *Ten? Five? I don't know.*

(Teacher points to each group in turn.)

T: One group, two groups, three groups. You've got three groups of two. And what did I need, do you remember? It was two groups of five, wasn't it?

C: *Ohhh.*

T: I need two groups of ...? How many in each group?

C: *Four.*

T: Two groups of five.

C: *Five.*

Building and drawing arrays can present difficulty for young children.

Here are some arrays. Which one shows two groups of five?

How might the use of a sentence frame support in such circumstances, e.g. ____ rows of ____

T: So, can somebody fill up my groups with five please?

C: *One, two, three, four, five!*

(Child counts out 5 counters.)

▲ A child adds 5 counters to make a second group of 5.

T: OK, there's one group of five, but I need two groups of five.

C: *One, two, three, four, five. Two groups of five.*

(Child counts out 5 more counters.)

T: So how many are there altogether?

C: *Ten.*

T: Good. So, can you have a go at drawing that array for me?

Sometimes children have difficultly 'holding onto' all the information in a task. What jottings could be made to help?

What next?

Set up a model of a 2 by 5 array with counters and cover this with a sheet of paper. Reveal the top row and quickly cover it again. How many were in the row? Move the paper to check, and quickly cover again. Reveal and then cover both rows. Can you find the total? Repeat, revealing the columns one at a time.

Going deeper

Set up an array with counters or draw it on paper. Cover the array with a sheet of paper. Reveal the objects in the top row only, and then reveal the objects in the left-hand column only. Can children work out the total from the partial information?

The teacher draws an array of 5 rows of 2 dots on a sheet of paper and covers it with another sheet without children seeing. The teacher reveals the top row briefly.

T: How many did you see?

C: *Two.*

(Teacher reveals the column of 5 dots and then re-covers.)

T: What about then?

C: *Five.*

T: So tell me about what is under the sheet. What groups do we have?

(Children discuss briefly.)

C: *We've got five groups of two.*

T: How do you know?

C: *Because there was two there at the top. And there must be five of them because there were five down the side.*

T: OK, great. And what does five groups of two equal?

C: *Ten.*

T: Good. So we've got five groups of two equals ten.

(Teacher rotates the whole array 90 degrees and covers again with paper.)

T: What about now? Has anything changed?

C: *There's still ten. But it's the other way round.*

T: Yes.

(Teacher reveals top row and re-covers.)

T: How many are here?

C: *Five.*

(Teacher reveals left-hand column and re-covers.)

> What does only revealing part of the array at a time encourage children to do?

> Notice how the teacher is providing experience of commutativity through rotating the array.

T: And here?

C: *Two.*

T: Yes. So, what is the same about the two arrays?

C: *They have ten counters.*

T: Good. What is different about them?

C: *That one's going straight and that one's going down.*

T: So, that one's going straight and that one's going down. But do we get to the same answer?

C: *Yes. That's five and two and that's two and five.*

T: So we've got two groups of five and five groups of two, and you get to the **same** answer.

> Use a sentence frame to record the arrays:
>
> ___ rows of ___ makes ___

What next?

Provide further drawings that show only the top row and left-hand column of arrays. Direct children to work out the total number of dots in each array, using cubes or counters to help them if needed.

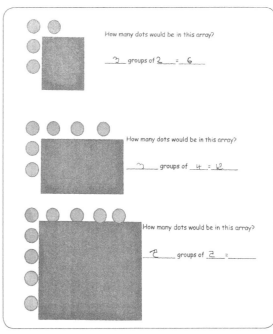

How many dots would be in this array?

___2___ groups of _2_ = _6_

How many dots would be in this array?

___3___ groups of _4_ = _12_

How many dots would be in this array?

___7___ groups of _2_ = ___

▲ A child visualizing the complete array from the clues provided.

Chapter 4
Fractions

Strand overview

Aims

Children develop their fluency when sharing in practical and concrete contexts; this builds on their play-based experience in Early Years Foundation Stage (EYFS). They solve problems involving halving and quartering: at first individual objects, countable groups and continuous quantities, and then abstract numbers and abstract quantities (e.g. time) by using concrete or pictorial representations of these. They reason about the similarities of the outcome each time – two or four equal parts – despite the differences in the methods used, such as sharing out, cutting up and pouring into. This leads to the introduction of formal language and fraction notation.

Key ideas

- With fractions, we must make equal parts. 'Sharing fairly' might mean something different to children in real life, e.g. an older sibling getting a larger slice of cake.

- The two or four equal parts need to be equivalent (e.g. in area, mass or quantity) but they can appear different and/ or be made up of smaller, separate parts (e.g. many cherries weighing the same as a few tangerines).

- Children need to consider regularly both 'non-examples' of halving or quartering where the resulting two or four parts are not equal (e.g. making equal depths of liquid when sharing a volume into different-shaped cups), and examples where the halving or quartering is exact but not obvious (e.g. making unequal depths when sharing a volume into different-shaped cups).

- Experiencing halving and quartering as processes prepares children for thinking about 'fraction of' as an abstract operation on numbers and the number line.

Models and apparatus

Children need experience of halving and quartering a wide variety of: single items ('fraction of 1') collections of discrete objects ('fraction of a group'); and lengths, masses and volumes ('fraction of a quantity'). They also need to see, describe and justify lots of examples of halving and quartering around them. Cumulatively, this gives them a broad base of examples for developing abstract understanding in Year 2.

 View the video on the Year 1 Teacher Support area of the Digital Planner

Progression through the National Curriculum

EYFS

- Automatically recall double facts up to 5 + 5.
- Compare sets of objects up to 10 in different contexts, considering size and difference.
- Explore patterns of numbers within numbers up to 10, including evens and odds.

Year 1

- Recognize, find and name a half as one of two equal parts of an object, shape or quantity.
- Recognize, find and name a quarter as one of four equal parts of an object, shape or quantity.

Year 2

- Recognize, find, name and write fractions $\frac{1}{3}$, $\frac{1}{4}$, $\frac{2}{4}$ and $\frac{3}{4}$ of a length, shape, set of objects or quantity.
- Write simple fractions for example, $\frac{1}{2}$ of 6 = 3 and recognize the equivalence of $\frac{2}{4}$ and $\frac{1}{2}$.

Year 1 sub-objectives

Term 2

- Recognize, find and name a half as one of two equal parts of an object, shape or quantity.
- Recognize, find and name a quarter as one of four equal parts of an object, shape or quantity.

Term 3

- Recognize, find and name a half as one of two equal parts of an object, shape or quantity.
- Recognize, find and name a quarter as one of four equal parts of an object, shape or quantity.

Tasks in Practice

Learning task 1: Breakfast time is juice time

DP Year 1 > Term 2 > Unit 10 > Fractions > Week 6 >
Learning task 1

In this task, children use concrete objects to solve problems about equal sharing of continuous quantities.

On track

Children who are 'on track' use the key words correctly when they describe and reason about the parts in relation to the whole. They correctly quarter the given quantities. They compare the cups (by eye) to ensure they have 4 equal quantities of juice.

> *Can you think of a time when it might be important to measure equally like this?*

Children are measuring out 'juice' fairly into four slightly different cups, using a measuring scoop.

T: It's tricky to make sure we're measuring equally, isn't it? What do we need to do?

C: *I need one scoop.*

(Teacher helps children add one scoop each to their cup.)

T: Have these two cups got the same amount?

C: *Yes.*

T: What about this next cup?

C: *One in there.*

(Child puts a scoop of juice into the cup.)

T: You did that very carefully, no spilling. Well done. What about this last cup?

C: *One in there.*

(Child adds a scoop.)

T: Have we finished?

C: *No, there's some juice left.*

T: Look at the size of the scoop and what we've got left. Are we going to have four more scoopfuls to share equally?

C: *No.*

T: What do you think you need to do?

C: *Put in a tiny bit.*

T: How will we make sure that it's still equal? Is there anything on the table you can use?

C: *This!*

(Child holds up a pipette.)

T: Why?

C: *Because we'll be able to get four of them in here.*

(Children take turns to use the pipette for each cup.)

T: Have you made sure you've done equal sharing?

C: *Yes. One squeeze in each.*

T: Are you going round again then?

(Children again take turns to use the pipette for each cup.)

T: Great, we've shared equally. But look at the cups. They look different.

C: *Yes, because that's higher.*

T: But you've shared it equally. So the cups all must have the same amount.

C: *My cup is bigger than his. That's why that one looks smaller than my one but we shared them equally.*

T: Good explanation. They look different because they're different cups. But did you share the juice into equal parts?

C: *Yes. We put two scoops and two squeezes in the cups. Four equal drinks!*

> The teacher reinforces the key idea that the amounts all have to be equal.

▲ Children sharing continuous measures fairly.

> *How could we record how much we have put in each cup?*

What next?

Children cut a length of string into quarters. Children compare the quartering of the string with the quartering of the juice. What is the same and what is different? Is one easier than the other? If so, why?

Needing support

Look and listen for children sharing a quantity into 2 or 4 pieces that are not equal. They know the parts must be equal but do not know how to achieve this, or they do not know that the parts must be equal, or they do not realize that their parts are not equal.

Children are guiding the teacher where to cut string into 4 equal parts.

T: Where do you want me to cut then?

C: *Here, in the middle.*

T: Right, let's have a look.

(Teacher makes one cut. The pieces of string are unequal in length.)

C: *We need two more! Here and here.*

T: Have we got four pieces?

C: *Yes.*

T: When we're sharing a cake, is it fair if we have some big pieces and some small ones?

C: *No, if you have a big slice of cake and mine is small. That's not fair.*

T: Right. So, have you got four equal pieces of string?

C: *No.*

T: Right, have a look again. Have a think about where to cut it first.

C: *Cut it there, in the middle.*

T: How do I know that this is the middle though?

C: *I can see.*

T: So I'm just going to guess that this is the middle then?

C: *Yes.*

T: Shall I cut it then? Is that two equal groups?

C: *No.*

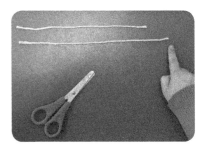

▲ Are the 2 pieces equal? Have we cut the string exactly in half?

> Be mindful of children who are content that the parts are unequal. Discussing fairness supports their understanding of equality.

> The teacher accepts the child's suggestion to help them realize why it is not the best solution, rather than immediately correcting it.

T: Let's try with another piece of string. Think about how you might find the middle exactly. What about if I fold it like this? (Teacher folds string in two, but not in half.) Does this make two equal pieces?

C: *No, this is longer.*

T: OK, can you fold it and make two equal pieces?

(Child does so.)

C: *Cut here.*

T: Good. So, how would I get four equal groups out of this string?

C: *Cut it in half again.*

T: Good. I want to see if you can now cut that string. What are you going to do?

C: *Fold it?*

T: Yes. Let's fold each piece in half again and cut each piece.

How has the teacher's modelling supported finding half?

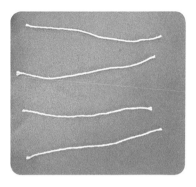

▲ A child uses folding to cut 4 equal pieces of string.

What next?

Ask children to use apparatus (e.g. a pan balance or a measuring scoop) to halve or quarter a quantity of something different (e.g. sand). Ask them to explain to you how they use the equipment to make sure each quantity is divided into 'fair shares'.

Going deeper

Ask children to cut two lengths of string or ribbon, or to draw two lines, so that half of one length (or line) is the same as a quarter of the other length (or line). They could do the same with two amounts of rice or sand.

A child has cut two lengths of string, one twice as long as the other.

T: Explain to me what you're doing with the string.

C: *I want half of this.* (Child holds up the shorter piece.) *So I'll fold it and show you half.*

(Child does so.)

T: What could we do to help us remember where the halfway point is?

(Child marks the halfway point using a pen.)

> The child is expressing an intuitive sense of a quarter being half of a half. How could you build on this?

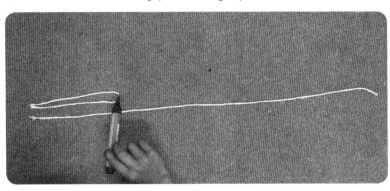

C: *I want one-quarter of this one.*

(Child holds up the longer piece.)

C: *I think it will be in the same place as half on the other one, but I need to check. I fold it once and then fold it again.*

(Child does so, and marks the quarter-way point using a pen.)

C: *I can compare them. Look, I've drawn in the same place on both of them.*

(Child lines up the ends of the two pieces of string, to show that the two pen marks also line up.)

> *Before you check, why do you think the quarter mark on the longer string will be in the same place as the half mark on the shorter string?*

T: So what can you say about your two pieces of string?

C: *Half of the shorter one is the same as a quarter of the longer one.*

T: How else could you describe the difference between the two pieces?

C: *The shorter string is half of the longer one.*

> Notice how this numberless problem is supporting the child to compare fractional relationships with different wholes.

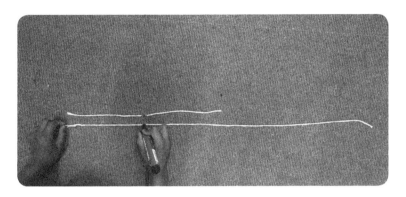

▲ Half of the shorter one is the same as a quarter of the longer one.

What next?

Show children two equal amounts of different juices. Label the first one 'half' and the second one 'quarter'.

Here is one half of the orange juice. What would all of the juice look like?

Repeat for one quarter of the apple juice. Why is there more apple juice than orange juice?

Tasks in Practice

Learning task 2: Halving and quartering 2-digit numbers

(DP) Year 1 > Term 3 > Unit 19 > Fractions > Week 9 > Learning task 2

In this task, children use base-ten apparatus concretely and pictorially to halve and quarter carefully chosen 2-digit numbers.

On track

Children who are 'on track' practically halve 42 and quarter 28, for example, and express the result in a written or spoken number sentence. When quartering 28, they describe how to share two 10-rods between four.

T: Can you show me one half of forty-two?

(Child places two 10-rods in each of two circles.)

T: Lovely, you've done your forty. And where's your two?

(Child places a 1-cube in each circle.)

T: Perfect, so what is one half of forty-two?

C: *Twenty-one.*

T: Brilliant, well done. Now, I would like you to quarter twenty-eight.

(Child builds 28 using two 10-rods and eight 1-cubes.)

T: Right, so we've got our twenty-eight. Can you quarter it by putting these into four equal parts? Have a go.

(Child shares the 8 ones out, two in each part, and holds up the tens.)

C: *I need to cut it in half.*

T: You need to cut those in half? Good. And if you could cut each rod in half, what would it be?

C: *Five.*

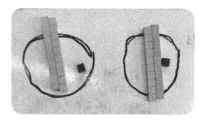

▲ Show me half of 42.

> The teacher uses the opportunity to revisit and consolidate children's work on place value met earlier in the year.

> The teacher subtly introduces the idea that we can talk about half as an amount but also as an action.

T: Fantastic. What are we going to do then? Can we do something with this?

(Teacher holds up a 10-rod.)

C: *This can be two fives?*

T: Have a go.

(Child replaces the two 10-rods with 4 groups of 5 ones and shares them equally so there are 7 ones in each circle.)

T: So, what is one-quarter of twenty-eight?

C: *Seven.*

T: Fantastic, can you make a picture and a sentence to show me?

(Child draws 4 circles with 7 dots in each, and writes $\frac{1}{4}$ of 28 is 7.)

T: Lovely.

What next?

Children share 42 then 44 then 46 counters between two. What do they notice about the numbers they are halving and the values of their halves? Can they predict half of 48 counters?

Needing support

Look and listen for children who distribute the 10-rods and 1-cubes into two logical but unequal groups, e.g. when sharing 26 they might make a group of the two 10-rods and a group of the six 1-cubes, or two groups each with four 'pieces' in them.

T: OK, we need to halve sixty-four. Can you make sixty-four?

(Child takes four 10-rods and four 1-cubes. They correctly split the four 1-cubes, putting two in each half.)

T: Okay, what's our number again? Can you say it for me?

C: *Sixty-four.*

T: Sixty-four, good. So, how many tens do you think sixty-four has?

C: *Hmm ... six tens?*

T: I think maybe six, shall we count them? What is this?

(Teacher holds up a 10-rod.)

T: This is a ...

C: *Ten.*

T: Ten, so we count in tens. Ten ...

C: *Twenty, thirty, forty. We need two more!*

T: That's it, well done, we need two more tens.

C: *Then it's equal, because one of the people would have three and the other would have three.*

(Child puts three 10-rods in each half.)

T: Three what? What are these?

(Teacher holds up a 10-rod.)

C: *Tens!*

T: Really good. So, what is one-half of sixty-four? How many have you got here?

(Teacher gestures at the 3 tens and 2 ones.)

C: *One, two, three, four, five. Five!*

(Child writes 5 under each half.)

Since children are working practically, the teacher chooses to work with quite a large number. This helps children with their work on place value, as well as halving.

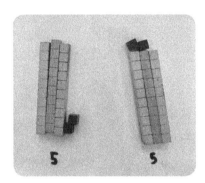

▲ A child demonstrates understanding of halves needing to be equal, but needs support in determining the value of the pieces.

Has the child misheard 'how many blocks have you got here?'

T: Five? Do you think? What is this?

(Teacher holds up a 10-rod.)

T: A ...?

C: *Ten!*

T: Ten, good. So, let's have a go.

C: *Ten, twenty, thirty, forty, fifty!*

(Child counts the 3 tens and 2 ones as a ten each.)

T: Fifty. So, do you think there's fifty there?

C: *Umm ... no. Because these are ones and that is ten!*

T: Oh, so what do we have to do then?

C: *Ten, twenty, thirty ...*

T: So, now we go into ones. Thirty ...

C: *Thirty-one, thirty-two.*

T: Good! So, can you change your answer?

(Child writes 32 under each half.)

> This task has highlighted that the child needs more practice in 'switching the count', namely, moving from counting in tens to counting in ones.

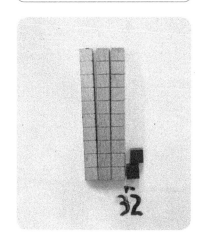

What next?

Ask children to share base-ten apparatus into equal groups. Ask: What is the same and what is different about rods and cubes? Can children move pieces from the high-value to the low-value group until they have two equal-value halves?

Going deeper

Children talk about what pattern(s) they observe in the numbers they are halving and quartering. They use their pattern(s) to predict the result of halving or quartering the next numbers and confirm (or not) their predictions using base-ten apparatus.

T: Can we share ninety shells between four sailors? Have a little explore and I'll come back.

(Children discuss the problem in a small group.)

T: So, have you managed to quarter ninety?

C: *Not yet. We're trying to.*

T: Good, so what's the problem?

C: *You can't quarter ten!*

T: You can't quarter ten? So, what have you done then?

C: *I've done twenties.*

T: So, you've put twenty in each quarter, so that's twenty, forty, sixty, eighty. And then you've tried to share your last ten out, so what have you done to your last ten?

C: *I've tried to quarter it.*

T: What number have you managed to quarter?

C: *Eight.*

T: So, can you quarter ninety?

C: *I don't think so.*

T: You can't quarter ninety and end up with a whole number, can you? What about ninety-two? Can you quarter ninety-two?

C: *I don't know.*

T: Well have a go, you're already on eighty-eight, so see if you can add some more to quarter ninety-two. How many do you think you need to add to eighty-eight to get to ninety-two?

C: *Four.*

T: Good, add four then.

(Child adds a one-dot to each quarter of his diagram.)

T: Good, did you manage to do that?

C: *Yes!*

> The teacher subtly reinforces the connection between 'share between four' and 'quartering'.

> The child implicitly suggests that 20 is a quarter of 80, which the teacher makes explicit.

T: Fantastic. What do you think the next number you'll be able to quarter is? You're on ninety-two, what do you think the next one's going to be?

C: *Ninety-four.*

T: Try ninety-four then.

(Child adds 2 one-dots.)

C: *Oh. No.*

T: No, you can't do ninety-four. So, what number do you think you will be able to do?

C: *Ninety-six.*

T: Ninety-six, good. How many do you have to add for there to be equal parts?

C: *Four.*

T: Good, so I could do eighty-eight and I could add four more and do ninety-two, and four more is ninety-six, and I could keep going. So, what do you think the next number I could quarter would be?

C: *One hundred.*

T: Exactly, so what do you have to do to quarter?

C: *You have to add one to each part. So add four each time.*

T: Well done! So you have spotted another pattern, haven't you?

Rather than question this suggestion, the teacher accepts it and invites the child to check it.

The teacher explicitly draws the children's attention to the fact that their answers are going up by four each time.

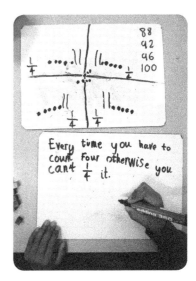

What next?

Children write or explain their discovered pattern for another child to test out.

Chapter 5
Geometry: properties of shapes

Strand overview

Aims

Children build on their prior experiences of exploring 2D and 3D shapes in the Early Years Foundation Stage (EYFS). They develop fluency in recognizing and naming 3D shapes and then 2D shapes, which they first identify as the faces of 3D shapes. They reason about sorting shapes into categories. In doing so, they describe similarities and differences between properties of shapes, such as the number of edges and vertices shapes have, and the number and nature of the faces of 3D shapes. They solve problems by using shape properties, such as identifying a 'mystery' 3D shape concealed in a bag.

Key ideas

- Children should explore 3D shapes first because 3D shapes actually exist in their world, whereas 2D shapes are an abstraction. Even models of 2D shapes will always have some depth, and so in reality they are examples of 3D shapes.

- The orientation of a shape does not change the type of shape that it is.

- 'Non-examples' (e.g. a triangle with curved sides) help children use language with increased precision: knowing 'what it is not' sharpens their knowledge of 'what it is'.

- Children should start to reason about shapes and their properties in general, e.g. all triangles have three straight edges and all cuboids have six plane faces, not just a particular triangle or a specific cuboid.

- Shapes also have important non-numerical properties: e.g. a cone, a sphere and a cylinder all roll, but they each do so in a different way.

Models and apparatus

Children need to handle shapes as often as possible, including examples of 'everyday' 3D shapes (e.g. cereal box, tennis ball). Touch is as important as sight (e.g. a rotated square face looks different but feels the same). Making impressions or prints of the faces of 3D shapes will make clear the 2D shapes that are the faces.

 View the video on the Year 1 Teacher Support area of the Digital Planner

Progression through the National Curriculum

EYFS

- Compare sets of objects up to 10 in different contexts, considering size and difference.

Year 1

- Recognize and name common 2D and 3D shapes, including:
  - 2D shapes, for example, rectangles (including squares), circles and triangles
  - 3D shapes, for example, cuboids (including cubes), pyramids and spheres.

Year 2

- Identify and describe the properties of 2D shapes, including the number of sides and line symmetry in a vertical line.

- Identify and describe the properties of 3D shapes, including the number of edges, vertices and faces.

- Identify 2D shapes on the surface of 3D shapes, [for example, a circle on a cylinder and a triangle on a pyramid].

- Compare and sort common 2D and 3D shapes and everyday objects.

Year 1 sub-objectives

Term 1

- Recognize and name common 3D shapes, including for example, cuboids (including cubes), and spheres.
- Recognize and name common 2D shapes, including for example, rectangles (including squares), circles and triangles.

Term 3

- Recognize and name common 3D shapes, including pyramids.
- Recognize and name common 2D shapes, including for example, rectangles (including squares), circles, hexagons and triangles.

Tasks in Practice

Learning task 1: Same or different?

(DP) Year 1 > Term 1 > Unit 3 > Geometry: properties of shapes > Week 7 > Learning task 1

In this task, children choose a criterion to sort shapes and label their results.

On track

Children who are 'on track' place shapes in and outside a sorting ring to show what is the same and what is different.

Pairs are given a sorting ring and a selection of 3D shapes, including cubes, cuboids and spheres, prisms, cylinders and cones.

T: You have got some shapes. I'd like you to sort your shapes. You're finding something that is the same and something that is ...?

C: *Different!*

T: All the shapes that are the same go in the hoop. Shapes that are different stay out of the hoop. So, you decide how you're going to sort them.

(Children put a cube, a cuboid, a triangular prism and a cylinder in their sorting ring.)

C: *These ones are the same. These have flat parts.*

T: Do all those shapes in there have flat surfaces?

C: *No. They do all have a flat surface but the sides aren't flat on this one.*

(Child picks up the cylinder.)

T: OK, we could sort them by flat faces and ... what are these?

(Teacher runs a finger around a curved surface.)

C: *Curved faces.*

> Keeping the task very open to start with helps assess what the children already focus on.

> The teacher takes the child's sorting criterion and passes it back to them to check.

T: Yes, these are called curved faces and these are called flat faces, aren't they?

C: *So everything in there will have a curved face.*

T: Good. And what about the ones outside the hoop?

C: *Flat faces.*

(Teacher holds up a cone.)

T: Can you tell me about this shape? Where would this shape go?

C: *In there.*

T: Well done. Are you happy with how you sorted them?

C: *Yes.*

T: Good. Can you find another way of sorting them?

▲ Those four shapes are the same, can you find any different shapes to put in your hoop?

What next?

Ask children how they could label their sorting rings.

Children might need support with the higher order skill of categorization after their sorting.

Needing support

Look and listen for children who remain focused only on the non-defining properties (colour, size, etc.) and not the defining properties (number of faces, vertices, etc.) of the shape.

T: So, you have sorted by colour.

C: *Yes, the shapes in the hoop are yellow.*

T: Can you show me another way to sort them? (Pause.) What is this shape called?

(Teacher holds up a red cuboid.)

C: *Cylinder.*

T: No, not a cylinder. This is a cylinder.

(Teacher holds up a red cylinder.)

T: What is this one called?

(Teacher holds up the red cuboid.)

C: *A rectangle?*

T: It does have a rectangle face.

(Teacher points to one of the cuboid's rectangle faces.)

T: But it has a different name.

C: *And it's got square bits.*

T: What is the name for the square bits? Do you remember?

C: *Edge?*

T: Try again!

C: *Face?*

T: Good. So, do you know what this shape is called?

C: *This is a boid ...*

T: A **cu**boid, yes. Have we got any more cuboids?

(Children point to more cuboids.)

T: What is the same about these?

C: *They've got squares here and rectangles here.*

T: Yes. Is there anything different about them?

C: *Colours?*

T: Yes, they are different colours aren't they?

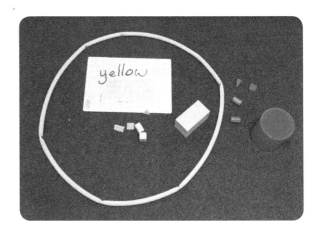

▲ The children have sorted by 'yellow shapes' and 'not yellow shapes' as their criterion. The teacher is supporting them to move back to sorting by property.

Can you explain what an edge is? How is it different to a face?

C: *And this one is really big.*

T: That's right. They are different sizes. But they are all still cuboids.

T: Can we sort them again, using what we have found out?

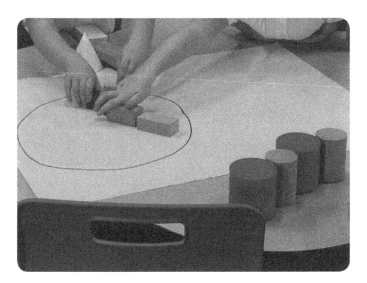

The teacher then supports the child as they look carefully at the properties of each shape to decide whether they are cuboids.

▲ Look at the shape of the faces. Can you sort the shapes that way instead?

What next?

Children compare two shapes, varying only one criterion at a time. What is the same? What is different? For example, a cube and sphere that are the same colour and similar sizes:

- the cube has flat faces, the sphere has one curved face.

- the cube has vertices, the sphere has no vertices.

- the cube has edges (all the same length), the sphere has no edges.

Going deeper

Show children two sorting rings containing shapes but no labels. They label the rings to show how they are the same and how they are different?

Children are shown two unlabelled sorting rings with shapes in, sorted by circular face and rectangular face.

T: How have these shapes been sorted?

C: *Circle and rectangle.*

(Teacher points at the 'circular face' ring.)

T: But this ring has both cylinders and cones. How come they can be together?

C: *Because they have the same face.*

T: What face is the same?

C: *That one and that one.*

(Child points to circular faces on cone and cylinder.)

T: What shape is this face?

C: *Circle.*

T: Circle face. Over here I can see cubes and cuboids. What's the same about them?

C: *They have faces that are rectangles.*

T: What a lovely sentence. Really good maths thinking today.

> We most often ask children to do the sorting first. How could the approach used here deepen children's understanding?

> *Could you sort the cubes and cuboids into two rings now? How would you label it?*

◄ Categorization is a higher order skill and can prove challenging. Allow time for discussion.

Going deeper

Children add more shapes to the rings, following the sorting criteria?

Children are shown two sorting rings with shapes in, sorted by flat faces and curved faces.

T: What's the same and what's different about these?

C: *These are all flat surfaces ...*

T: What's the word we use for this?

C: *Face.*

T: Well done.

C: *These ones have a flat face, and these have curved faces.*

T: Can you write labels for the rings?

(Children write labels.)

T: Where would you put this shape? Flat faces or curved faces?

(Teacher holds up a dice.)

C: *Flat faces.*

T: Good, can you put it in there?

(Child puts the dice in the 'flat faces' ring.)

T: Can you sort this one?

(Teacher holds up a pyramid.)

(Child goes to put it in the 'curved face' ring.)

T: Have a think about that one. Has it got flat faces or curved faces?

C: *Flat faces.*

(Child puts it in the 'flat faces' ring.)

T: Good. Could you find another way to sort these shapes?

> Show me the flat faces and the curved faces. How do they feel different?

What next?

Ask children to think of different ways to sort the shapes. How would they change the labels?

Tasks in Practice

Learning task 3: Puzzling pyramids and prisms

DP Year 1 > Term 3 > Unit 16 > Geometry: properties of shapes > Week 4 > Learning task 3

In this task, children compare pyramids and prisms to establish why a pyramid is not a prism.

On track

Children who are 'on track' describe the similarities and differences between pyramids and prisms, e.g. a prism always has two identical shaped bases, one at the top and one at the bottom. But a pyramid always has an apex at the top instead of a second base.

▲ Children tell the teacher how many faces and bases to draw for each prism and pyramid.

The teacher has guided the class through exploring the differences between pyramids and prisms, including drawing around the faces.

T: How are a pyramid and a prism different?

C: *A pyramid has one base and a prism has two bases.*

T: Great thinking. Can you show me?

(Child gathers four shapes: a triangular-based pyramid, a square-based pyramid, a triangular prism and a cuboid.)

C: *These two are pyramids – they have one base.*

(Child places the two pyramids together.)

C: *These two are prisms – they have two bases.*

(Child places the triangular prism and cuboid together, each standing on one of its bases.)

T: Nice explanation. So, is this a prism or a pyramid?

(Teacher holds up the triangular prism.)

C: *Prism.*

T: How do you know?

C: *It has two bases.*

> When a child offers a correct answer, how and when might you prompt them to provide justification?

T: What kind of prism is it?

C: *Triangular-based prism.*

T: How do you know it's a triangular prism?

C: *It has two triangles as bases.*

(Child points to the two triangular bases.)

T: And this?

(Teacher holds up square-based pyramid.)

C: *Pyramid. Square-based pyramid.*

T: How do you know?

C: *It has one base which is a square.*

T: What else does a pyramid have? Can you remember that word I used?

(Teacher points to the top of the pyramid.)

C: *Apex.*

T: Good remembering, well done.

> How can you probe for more complete naming of shapes, and model the correct language where needed?

> If the child had not taken on board the correct word here, what could you do to embed the terminology?

What next?

Children complete the worksheet from the Digital Planner, showing the shapes of the bases and other faces of four shapes: a square prism (cuboid), a square-based pyramid, a hexagonal prism and a hexagonal-based pyramid.

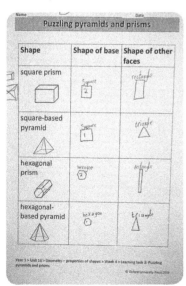

◀ A child has drawn the shapes of the faces and identified the number of bases for each shape, but has not yet indicated the number of other faces.

Needing support

Look and listen for children who focus only on the shape of the bases and faces when comparing, and do not talk about the number of bases. Also, look and listen for children who confuse faces and bases.

The teacher shows children a square prism and a square-based pyramid.

T: Who can tell me the difference between these? Think about using the word 'base'.

C1: *That one has a rectangle* (child points to prism) *and that one has a square* (child points to pyramid) *and rectangles and squares are not the same.*

T: Yes, some of the faces are different shapes. They both have a square face, but the prism also has rectangles, and the pyramid has triangles. What else makes a prism and a pyramid different?

C2: *Is it because the base is different?*

T: It does have something to do with the base.

(Teacher gives each child a shape, and lays out some sticky notes with 'base' written on.)

T: Can you find the bases on your shapes? When you find a base, put a sticky note on it.

(Child 1 selects two sticky notes.)

T: Why do you need two?

C1: *Because it has two bases.*

T: Good. And what shape is it? What shape has two bases?

C1: *A prism?*

T: Fantastic, it's a prism. And what's the shape of its base?

C1: *A hexagon.*

T: So we call it a ...

C1: *Hexagon-based prism.*

T: Great, a hexagonal prism. I see you have two sticky notes too. Do you know what your shape is?

C3: *Triangle-based prism.*

> When a child is starting to move towards the answer you are looking for, how can you take what they have said and build on it?

> How does physically labelling the bases help to focus children's attention?

T: Fantastic, a triangular prism.

(Teacher draws two sorting rings, and labels them 'one base'/'pyramid' and 'two bases'/'prism'.)

T: Can you put your shapes in the right rings?

(Children start to sort their shapes.)

T: Tell me about prisms: how many bases does a prism have?

C2: One?

T: Use this to help you.

(Teacher points to the labelled sorting rings.)

T: A prism has how many bases?

C2: Two?

T: Good, and how many bases does a pyramid have?

C2: One.

T: How many bases does your shape have?

C2: One.

T: One base. So what are we going to call it? One base, is it a pyramid or a prism?

C2: It's a pyramid.

T: A pyramid, well done. Can you put it in the right ring?

(Child 2 places square-based pyramid in the 'pyramid' ring.)

T: Well done, good job.

> *Can you convince me that your prism has two bases?*

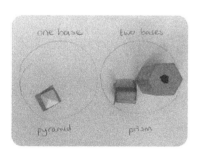

◀ Children use sticky notes with 'base' written on to label the bases on each shape, and then sort them.

What next?

Ask children to stick 'face' sticky notes to the shapes' faces. They should realize that every face will need a 'face' sticky note, and that some faces will also be labelled 'base'. Can they describe the number of faces and bases each shape has?

Going deeper

Show children an image of the Egyptian pyramids. Say: Juliet comes back from her holiday to Egypt and thinks that real pyramids can only have a square base. Do you agree? Mario thinks that a cone is another type of pyramid. Do you agree? Convince me of your answers.

T: Juliet went on holiday to Egypt to see the real pyramids and she took this photo. She thinks that pyramids must have a square base. Is she right? What do you think?

C: *I think it's true, but I don't know why.*

T: Well, let's have a look.

(Teacher shows a hexagonal-based pyramid.)

T: Does this pyramid have a square base?

C: *No.*

T: How do you know?

C: *Because the angles are too big.*

T: The angles are too big? What angles?

C: *The bottom angles. The bits where they meet together.*

T: Good, so you're saying that bigger angles on the base means it has more sides. Juliet says that these pyramids (teacher points to photo) **are the only types of pyramid because they've got a square base.** Is that true?

C: *No. The real ones in Egypt are square but they're not the only kind of pyramid.*

T: How do you know?

C: *It's because there's different kinds of ones, like this one.*

(Child points to the hexagonal-based pyramid.)

T: Good. And what's that one called?

C: *A hexagonal-based pyramid.*

T: Perfect, lovely.

▲ A child points to the angles on the base of the hexagonal pyramid.

(Teacher shows a cone.)

T: And this – is this a pyramid?

C: *No, this is a cone. The base has a curved edge, so it doesn't have a polygon base. It can't be called a pyramid because a circle's not a polygon, and the surfaces aren't all flat.*

T: Why do you think it needs a polygonal base?

C: *Because I know a prism has to have polygonal faces, so I think a pyramid does too. A cylinder can't be called a circular prism because a circle is not a polygon.*

T: That's really good reasoning. What is the same about a cone and a pyramid?

C: *They both have one base and an apex.*

T: And what is different?

C: *A cone doesn't have polygonal faces.*

T: Good reasoning and exploring, well done.

What next?

Ask children to discuss whether or not a cube is a prism.

> How does the introduction of the cone challenge children to think more deeply about pyramids?

> *Could you come up with a definition of a pyramid, that would be true for any type of pyramid?*

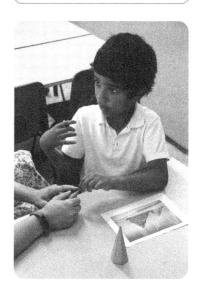

▲ A child points to the apex of a cone.

Chapter 6
Measurement

Strand overview

Aims

Children build on their experience in the Early Years Foundation Stage (EYFS). They measure to solve problems comparing quantities that cannot be counted (e.g. they can't 'count' two ribbons to decide which is longer). They develop fluency comparing lengths, masses and volumes using 'classroom units' (e.g. cubes and paper clips), and then start to do so using standard metric units. They become familiar with coins and their values, and reason about simple equivalences of coins (e.g. that two 5ps are worth the same as one 10p). They solve problems about time; they 'tell the time' when events occur, and they put events in sequence.

Key ideas

- Equivalence underpins measuring: how many cubes are equivalent to the length of the book? If two objects have, say, different masses then each will be equivalent to a different number of identical cubes. We need to use repeated, identical units to be certain of this conclusion.

- Measuring is necessary when the quantities being compared are not physically close or adjacent, or they are being measured at different times.

- Equivalence in money is not physical; one small coin can be equivalent to several larger coins.

- Learning to 'tell the time' does not develop children's sense of the passage and duration of time.

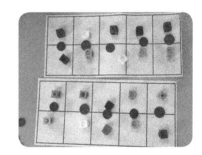

Models and apparatus

For length, mass and volume, work practically as much as possible, using everyday items, so children can get a 'feel' for these measures. Measuring with multiple copies of the unit is simpler, both practically and cognitively, than using one unit repeatedly, but both should be practised. Holding small, heavy objects and large, light ones can help children to distinguish between mass and volume. Handling real coins familiarizes children with their appearance. Analogue clocks with movable hands are helpful when starting to learn to tell the time, but children also need to see the hands moving in real time to develop their understanding of duration.

 View the video on the Year 1 Teacher Support area of the Digital Planner

Progression through the National Curriculum

EYFS

- Compare sets of objects up to 10 in different contexts, considering size and difference.

Year 1

- Compare, describe and solve practical problems for:
  - lengths and heights (for example, long/short, longer/shorter, tall/short, double/half)
  - mass/weight (for example, heavy/light, heavier than, lighter than)
  - capacity and volume (for example, full/empty, more than, less than, half, half full, quarter)
  - time (for example, quicker, slower, earlier, later).
- Measure and begin to record the following:
  - lengths and heights
  - mass/weight
  - capacity and volume
  - time (hours, minutes, seconds).

- Recognize and know the value of different denominations of coins and notes.
- Sequence events in chronological order using language (for example, before and after, next, first, today, yesterday, tomorrow, morning, afternoon and evening).
- Recognize and use language relating to dates, including days of the week, weeks, months and years.
- Tell the time to the hour and half past the hour and draw the hands on a clock face to show these times.

Year 2

- Choose and use appropriate standard units to estimate and measure length/height in any direction (m/cm); mass (kg/g); temperature (°C); capacity (litres/ml) to the nearest appropriate unit, using rulers, scales, thermometers and measuring vessels.
- Compare and order lengths, mass, volume/capacity and record the results using >, < and =.
- Recognize and use symbols for pounds (£) and pence (p); combine amounts to make a particular value.

- Find different combinations of coins that equal the same amounts of money.
- Solve simple problems in a practical context involving addition and subtraction of money of the same unit, including giving change.
- Compare and sequence intervals of time.
- Tell and write the time to five minutes, including quarter past/to the hour and draw the hands on a clock face to show these times.
- Know the number of minutes in an hour and the number of hours in a day.

Year 1 sub-objectives

Term 1

- Compare, describe and solve practical problems for lengths and heights (for example, higher/lower, long/short, longer/shorter, tall/short, taller/shorter, double/half).
- Measure and begin to record lengths and heights.
- Sequence events in chronological order using language (for example, before and after, next, first, today, yesterday, tomorrow, morning, afternoon and evening).
- Recognize and use language relating to dates including days of the week, weeks, months and years.

Term 2

- Compare, describe and solve practical problems for mass/weight (for example, heavy/light, heavier than, lighter than).
- Compare, describe and solve practical problems for time (for example, quicker, slower, earlier, later).
- Measure and begin to record mass/weight.
- Measure and begin to record time (hours, minutes, seconds).
- Recognize and know the value of different denominations of coins and notes.
- Sequence events in chronological order using language (for example, before and after, next, first, today, yesterday, tomorrow, morning, afternoon and evening).
- Recognize and use language relating to dates, including days of the week, weeks, months and years.
- Tell the time to the hour and half past the hour and draw the hands on a clock face to show these times.

Term 3

- Compare, describe and solve practical problems for capacity and volume (for example, full/empty, more than, less than, half, half full, quarter).
- Measure and begin to record lengths and heights.
- Measure and begin to record capacity and volume.

Tasks in Practice

Learning task 3: How far can you throw?

(DP) Year 1 > Term 1 > Unit 5 > Measurement > Week 10 > Learning task 3

In this task, children solve the problem of comparing distances that cannot be compared directly.

On track

Children who are 'on track' confidently use comparative and superlative words to describe length relationships.

Children have thrown three bean bags (red, green and blue) from different starting points marked with masking tape.

T: Which bean bag has been thrown the furthest?

C1: The blue one is the furthest.

T: Why do you think that?

C1: Because the start line is further back from the other lines?

T: Do we agree or disagree?

C2: I agree.

T: Why do you agree?

C2: The blue one started a bit lower.

T: What do you mean by lower?

C2: A bit more behind.

T: The starting line is further back, yes, lovely. Which bean bag do you think has been thrown the shortest distance? And why?

C3: The red. It's close to the green, but he was further forward than us when he threw the red.

T: Well done. Let's check it. I've got some string here. Could you use this to compare the distances? Why don't you start with the blue?

(Children measure the distance from the tape to the blue bean bag and cut the piece of string.)

> What are the benefits of asking children to justify why they agree or disagree with each other?

> How can you probe for clarification when children use imprecise language, without leading them too much?

C3: The length of the string is the same distance as the blue bean bag.

T: Great explanation. Let's use the string to try and prove that the green one went a shorter distance. What do you think will happen?

C2: The string won't be as long because this one's even shorter.

T: Can you measure to check? Where are you going to hold the piece of string?

C1: On the tape where the throw started.

(Children use the string to measure from the tape to the green bean bag and mark it with green pen.)

T: Let's do the same thing for the red.

(Children use the string to measure from the tape to the red bean bag and mark it with red pen.)

T: Now we've got our string with the marks on, how can we use that to tell us which bean bag was thrown the shortest distance?

(Children compare the marks on the string.)

C3: The red one's shorter, because the green one's start was further back.

T: And how does the string help us to know this?

C3: We can measure all the distances along one line.

T: That makes it easier to compare, doesn't it?

> Do children understand the need for a baseline when measuring distance? If not, how could you respond?

▲ Children cut a piece of string the length of their longest throw and then mark the distance of the other throws on the string to compare.

What next?

Ask children to use one long non-standard unit of measure to decide whether another length is longer or shorter, e.g. use a long stick to decide if the door is wider than the bookcase.

Needing support

Look and listen for children who consider the landing point of the bean bag and not the starting point, so think that the bean bag that landed the furthest away is the longest throw.

Children stand on different start lines and throw their bean bags. Red is thrown the shortest distance, then blue, then green.

T: Which do you think has been thrown the shortest distance?

C: *The blue has been thrown the shortest distance.*

T: What makes you think that?

C: *Because it's behind.*

T: OK. We have to think about if something's close to you or far away from you, don't we? We're going to have a go at measuring the distance of each throw and see if you're right. I want you to measure yours with pigeon steps. So you're going to take steps like this.

(Teacher demonstrates walking heel to toe. Child starts taking steps from the bean bag.)

T: Where do you start from each time to make it fair? Where did you stand to throw from?

(Children point to the start tape.)

T: Yes, so we need to measure from the tape.

(Child takes pigeon steps from the tape to the red bean bag.)

T: Lovely ... one, two, three, four and a bit. Let's record red as four steps.

(Another child starts to take pigeon steps towards the next bean bag.)

T: Will it be fair if we compare your steps to his steps?

C: *No.*

T: Why not?

C: *His feet might be bigger or smaller.*

T: Good, so he should do all the steps, and you help count. Can you try the next one then?

C: *One, two, three, four, five, six, seven. Seven and a bit.*

> What are the benefits of asking children to use their own feet to measure and compare the distances?

> How might you probe this answer further?

T: Lovely, shall we record that? Green is seven. What's the blue one?

(Child takes 5 pigeon steps to the blue bean bag.)

◀ Children take 'pigeon steps' to measure the distance each bean bag was thrown.

If the distances travelled by the blue and red bean bags had been too similar to be compared using pigeon steps, what could you suggest children try next?

T: So green is seven steps, blue is five steps and red is four steps. You said you thought that the blue one had been thrown the shortest distance. Do you agree or disagree?

C: *I've changed my mind and disagree. I think red is the shortest.*

T: OK. Do you agree that red was thrown the shortest distance?

C: *Yes.*

How is it helpful to ask children to look back on their initial assumptions, and compare them to what they have now discovered?

T: Good. And which was thrown the longest distance or the furthest?

C: *Green.*

T: Why did we think blue was the shortest before we measured?

C: *I started closer.*

T: That's right, you started further forward. Well done.

What next?

Ask children to measure with string, taking care to start on the start line. Use one piece of string for each bean bag so they can line them up and compare them after.

Going deeper

Challenge children to find out which is the longer of two lengths around the classroom. For example: Which is longer – the desk or the bookcase?

T: I want to know which is longer: the rug, or that blue bottom on the whiteboard stand? But you can't move the rug next to the board. So, firstly, can you estimate which one do you think is longer?

C: *The whiteboard stand.*

T: Why?

C: *I think it's got an extra bit.*

T: How could we check? You're not allowed to use a ruler!

C1: *Wool!*

C2: *Glue sticks!*

T: Shall we try glue sticks?

(Children lay glue sticks along the side of the rug.)

> Can you show me what you mean by 'an extra bit'?

◀ Children use glue sticks to measure the length of the rug.

> In what other ways could children record their measurements? What recording suggestions might they come up with for themselves?

C: *One, two, three, four, five … It's nearly six. But I think we have to take the lid off. It's not a whole glue stick.*

T: Can you record a tally?

C: *I think I'll put six down as it's so close.*

T: OK, you've rounded the length up to six. Fine. Now let's see how many the bottom of the whiteboard stand is.

(Children lay glue sticks along the base of the whiteboard stand.)

◄ Children use glue sticks to measure the bottom of the whiteboard stand.

How would you decide whether it is appropriate to introduce the language of rounding to this group of children?

C: *It's six and about three quarters. It's nearly seven. I'm going to say seven.*

T: Lovely, so you're rounding up to seven. Can you record it?

(Children record.)

Could you record the length to the nearest quarter? Would this be more accurate than using tally marks?

LHII
carpet = 6 glue sticks
White board stander = 7 glue sticks
    our prediction was right
The white board stander was longer

T: Were you correct in your predictions?

C: *Yes. The rug was almost six sticks and the whiteboard stand was nearly seven. I thought it would be longer, though.*

What next?

Ask children to measure their chosen items again using another unit of measure.

Tasks in Practice

Learning task 5: Can you make?

DP Year 1 > Term 2 > Unit 8 > Measurement > Week 2 > Learning task 5

In this task, children use coins and cubes to model the value of a certain coin.

On track

Children who are 'on track' count in ones, twos, fives and tens to decide how many coins they need to make a larger total. Children work systematically to find possible combinations of coins to make 20p and 50p.

Children connect 20 cubes and try to model the value with coins.

T: Has anybody found another way to make 20 pence using different coins?

C: *Ten 2 pences.*

T: How did you find out that was 20 pence, what did you count in?

C: *We counted in twos.*

T: OK, so ten 2 pences. Anybody find a different way to using 2 pences?

C: *Five and five and five and five. Four fives!*

T: What did you count in to get to twenty?

C: *Fives.*

T: Shall we count in fives? Five ... if you had two fives together what would you have?

C: *Ten.*

T: Five, ten ...

C: *Fifteen, twenty!*

T: Any other ways? We found four 5 pences. We've had ten 2 pences.
   Is there another way to make it?

> The teacher subtly reinforces that counting in fives is the same as adding five.

> *So four 5ps make 20p and two 10ps also make 20p. Why are there more 5ps than 10ps that make 20p?*

▲ Making 20p

C: *Ten and ten.*

T: How many 10 pence coins did you need?

C: *Two.*

T: Has anybody found a different way to make twenty?

C: *One two, eight ones and one ten.*

T: A combination of coins, interesting. I like it. Great thinking.

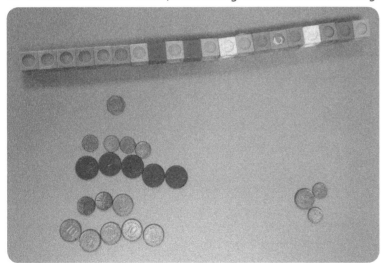

> If I take this 10p away, how could you use other coins to replace it and still make 20p?

▲ Exploring different ways to make 20p

What next?

Children work systematically to show as many of the coin combinations for 20 as they can. Encourage them to use known number facts to help them, e.g. I know that double 10 is 20, so I think you need two 10p coins to make 20p.

Needing support

Look and listen for children who work randomly through the different coins to make totals, so find it difficult to keep track of whether they have all the possibilities, and those who struggle to step count to a larger total.

This child is finding combinations to make 20p. She has already done two 10p coins, and the group have looked at 1p coins and 2p coins.

T: You can use different coins. You don't just have to use the same coin.

C: *I'm using the same coins because I don't really know how to add different coins. The reason why I get confused is because when they are the same colour, I start to think they are the same number and then I get confused.*

T: OK, how do you know they're not the same coin?

C: *Because it says ten on.*

T: It does, doesn't it? Well what if we add a 10 pence and a 5 pence together. Could we use our cubes to help us?

C: *Yes.*

T: What's this one?

C: *10 pence.*

T: How many cubes will we need?

C: *Ten.*

(Child makes a tower of 10 cubes.)

C: *Then I'm going to write a plus sign.*

T: Good idea. You've got ten. What number are we going to add to it?

(Child starts making another tower of cubes.)

T: What are you adding now?

C: *Five.*

T: How many do we have altogether?

(Child starts counting the cubes in ones.)

> The teacher might note to provide further space and time for children with limited experience of coins and notes to sort and explore them.

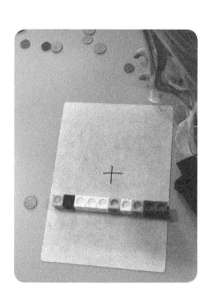

T: Do we need to start from one? We know this is a tower of ten, so what could we do?

(Child starts from ten and counts on the five additional cubes.)

C: *Fifteen.*

T: What can we do to make twenty? Do you need any more?

C: *Yes. I mean no, we need less.*

T: Shall we use 10-frames? That might help.

(Child places the 15 cubes on two 10-frames.)

T: How many have you got altogether?

C: *Ten, twenty ... no, ten, eleven, twelve, thirteen, fourteen, fifteen.*

T: We need to make a total of twenty. What do we need to do?

C: *We need to add some more ones.*

T: OK.

C: *So I would take ...*

(Child starts adding cubes to the second 10-frame to make twenty.)

T: How many have you got now?

C: *Twenty. That was five that I just added on. So, we had ten and then we added five and then we added five.*

T: Brilliant. Can you show me those coins?

(Child places a 10p and two 5p coins in a line.)

T: That's a lovely way to make twenty.

> How confident might children need to be in counting in fives before being given this task?

What next?

Children swap coins to find another way to make twenty, e.g. swap a 5p for five 1ps.

> A further step would be to show children how we can replace 10p for two 5ps and we still have 20p.

Going deeper

Ask: What is the smallest and greatest number of coins you can use to make a total of 50p?

T: What's your total in 2 pences?

C: *One, two, three ... twenty-five! Twenty-five 2 pence coins.*

T: Twenty-five! So what's the value of all those coins altogether?

C: *Fifty!*

T: Fantastic, 50 pence. What's the largest amount of coins you needed to use to make fifty? Look at your totals. What coins did you have to use the most of?

C: *Twos!*

T: 2 pence coins. What about the smallest number of coins?

C: *One!*

T: Fantastic. Is there another way to make 50 pence using lots of coins?

C: *Ones.*

T: And how many 1 pence coins will you need?

C: *Fifty!*

> How might asking the child how they knew the answer was 50 so quickly help deepen their understanding?

> Where might you take this task with such a confident child?

▲ Ways to make 50p

Going deeper

Ask: Is it possible to make 50p with one coin, two coins, three coins, four coins, five coins, and so on?

T: We're trying to make 50 pence. Look at all of your lovely coins you've got there. Can you only use two coins?

C: *No.*

T: OK, can you use three coins to make fifty?

C: *Um, yes. Two twenties and a ten.*

T: Good! Can you use one coin to make 50 pence?

C: *Yes.*

T: Which one?

C: *Fifty!*

T: Can you use four coins to make 50 pence?

C: *Yes. Ten, twenty, ten and ten.*

T: What about five coins?

C: *10 pences.*

T: How many 10 pence coins to make fifty?

C: *Five.*

> Can you explain why you can't use only two coins?

> How many ways of making 50p with five coins can you find?

▲ Five 10p coins on 5 cubes to make 50p

What next?

Is it possible to make one pound using one coin, two coins, three coins, four coins, five coins, and so on?

Tasks in Practice

Learning task 1: Baby Bear's new bowl

 Year 1 > Term 3 > Unit 17 > Measurement > Week 5 >
Learning task 1

In this task, children establish which of two containers holds the most by using lots of the same unit to measure and compare.

On track

Children who are 'on track' fill and count a single unit (container) multiple times to measure and compare capacity.

Children are given two bowls with similar but different capacities, each full of sand or rice. They are also given a number of identical sized cups.

T: So, Mummy Bear wants to buy the bowl that can hold the most porridge. How could we use the cups to help us to decide which bowl holds more?

C: *Pour the sand into cups and see which bowl has the most?*

T: Good! Let's try that.

(Children carefully scoop and tip sand from the bowls into the cups, to measure and compare the capacity of the bowls.)

T: So, which bowl should Mummy Bear buy? Which bowl holds the most cups?

C: *That one.*

(Child points to the white bowl.)

T: Why?

C: *It's because that one* (child points to white bowl) *has half and a whole. But this one* (child points to blue bowl) *only has one cup.*

T: Okay, so you think Mummy Bear should buy the white bowl. Brilliant.

> It is easier for children to fill the bowl and empty into cups than to count the cups needed to fill the bowl.

> *How could we record how much each bowl holds so we don't forget?*

▲ Which bowl holds the most cups of sand?

What next?

Children try the task with smaller cups and bigger bowls.
How can you keep track of how many cups each bowl holds?
Ask children to discuss their different suggestions for how
to do this. For example, collect one cube per cup or use
tally marks.

Needing support

Look and listen for children who don't fill the units (containers) completely when measuring capacity.

T: Which bowl should Mummy Bear buy? Which bowl holds the most?

C: *That one* (child points to white bowl) *got two, and that one* (child points to purple bowl) *got two.*

T: But what's the problem with these cups?

(Teacher points to the two cups by the purple bowl.)

T: Are both cups full?

C: *No.*

T: So, can we say there's two cups there?

C: *No.*

T: So, do you think you can make one of those full and see what you're left with? How could you make one of them full?

C: *Um, so we used lots on that one and a little bit on that one.*

T: Yes, but look how full their cup is.

(Teacher points to another pair's cup.)

T: Could you see if you could make that one full? What could you do?

C: *Add some rice from this cup.*

(Child goes to pour rice from the fuller cup into the emptier cup.)

T: Yes, but why don't you use this cup (teacher points to the emptier cup) **to pour into this cup** (teacher points to the fuller cup), **so you have less to pour?**

(Child does so.)

T: How many cups do you have now?

C: *Two cups.*

T: Are those two cups full?

▲ If cups aren't all full, consider asking children to order the cups from fullest to emptiest.

▲ How could you make that cup full?

C: This one is.

(Child points to full cup.)

T: What's different about this cup?

(Teacher points to not-full cup.)

C: It's not all the way full.

T: What would you say then? How much is in there?

C: One?

T: Well no, the full cup would be one. How much is in this one compared to that one?

C: A tiny bit?

T: Can you think about using your fractions?

C: Half?

T: Half! Yes. So does this bowl hold the most?

C: No.

T: So what did we say? It holds one cup and a ...?

C: Half.

T: And why is this bowl the smaller one? How many cups did that one have?

(Teacher points to the white bowl.)

C: Two.

T: So, which one do you think holds the most?

C: That one.

(Child points to the white bowl.)

T: Right, good working out.

> *Think about why it could be confusing if we said this cup was one.*

> Children could mark halfway on the cups to support this.

What next?

Ask children to pour juice into three identical cups. If they pour unevenly, take the full cup, leaving children the cups with less juice. Why isn't that fair?

Going deeper

Provide children with a third bowl and the following problem: Mummy Bear sees another bowl that Baby Bear might like, and now she can't decide which of the three bowls would hold the most porridge. Could you help? Which bowl holds the least? The most? Challenge children to just use one cup for measuring.

Children have measured the capacity of the new bowl, and compared it to the other two bowls.

▲ Which bowl held the most? You could use counters to help you keep track.

T: Right, so which bowl have you decided that Mummy Bear should buy now?

C: *That one.*

(Child points to the new bowl.)

T: Why?

C: *Because that one holds the most. Four and a half.*

T: Four and a half, OK. And which one held the least?

C: *That one.*

(Child points to the smallest bowl.)

T: Why?

C: *Because it holds less than one cup. Half a cup.*

T: So, what did you have to do when you were measuring?

C: *We had to get it all the way to the top.*

T: So, each cup had to be full?

C: *Yes, but sometimes there was a bit more than a full cup left over.*

T: How did you keep track of your cups?

C: *We used counters. One counter for whole cups and we wrote the half cups down.*

T: Good. And how many did that middle bowl hold?

C: *One cup.*

> How is the use of a benchmark measure (i.e. the cup) supporting predictions about capacity?

T: And did you get your predictions right for how many cups this new bowl held?

C: *Hmm ... no.*

T: Nearly though. How many did you say?

C: *I said four, Jamie said five and Rosa said six.*

T: So, it was between you and Jamie then? Lovely!

> *Let's look at our predictions. Whose was closest to the answer? If we carry out the problem again with different bowls will someone else get the closest prediction?*

▲ How many cups did you estimate would be in the bowl?

What next?

Fill one of the smaller bowls to the top and pour into the largest bowl. Can you work out how many more cupfuls you would need to add to the biggest bowl to make it full? Estimate how many you will need first.

◀ How will you keep track of the cups of sand you add to fill the bowl?

Strand overview

Aims

Children build on their prior experience of describing position, direction and movement, gained in the Early Years Foundation Stage (EYFS). They develop fluency with the language conventionally used to do so, in particular giving and following instructions (e.g. make a half-turn; take 3 steps to the left; stand behind the red chair), describing relative positions (e.g. the car is outside the shop) and comparative positions (e.g. the bird is above the tree but below the aeroplane), and specifying movement (e.g. the teacher is walking towards the door; the dancer is making a half turn). They use this language to give their reasoning when solving problems about position and direction, e.g. locating an object on a grid they can't see, when given information from someone who can see it.

Key ideas

- Children need to 'act out' the language of position, direction and movement to develop their spatial awareness and reasoning.

- Shared language and agreed conventions enable one person to describe the position, direction and movement of objects to another person, even when the objects are not visible to that person.

- Doing this in lessons develops the fluency of children's reasoning with mental images: their 'seeing in the mind's eye'.

- Sometimes, knowing the comparative position of one object tells us the position of another (e.g. if the bird is above the tree and below the aeroplane, we know that the aeroplane must be above the tree), but sometimes it does not (e.g. the car can be outside the shop and the dog can be outside the car, but the dog might not be outside the shop).

Models and apparatus

Children need lots of opportunities to position and move themselves as well as concrete objects. An analogue clock with movable hands will be useful for modelling quarter, half and three-quarter turns.

 View the video on the Year 1 Teacher Support area of the Digital Planner

Progression through the National Curriculum

EYFS
- Compare sets of objects up to 10 in different contexts, considering size and difference.

Year 1
- Describe position, direction and movement, including whole, half, quarter and three-quarter turns.

Year 2
- Order and arrange combinations of mathematical objects in patterns and sequences.

- Use mathematical vocabulary to describe position, direction and movement, including movement in a straight line and distinguishing between rotation as a turn and in terms of right angles for quarter, half and three-quarter turns (clockwise and anti-clockwise).

Year 1 sub-objectives

Term 2

- Describe position and direction.
- Describe movement including whole, half, quarter and three-quarter turns.

Tasks in Practice

Learning task 1: Searching for counters

(**DP**) Year 1 > Term 2 > Unit 11 > Geometry: position and direction > Week 7 > Learning task 1

In this task, children play a 'behind the screen' game, and use positional language to locate their partner's counters.

On track

Children who are 'on track' describe a specific square in a grid using positional language accurately, e.g. The middle square on the bottom row. They correctly identify a square when a question is asked about it using positional language, e.g. Is there a counter in the left square of the top row?

Child 2 has secretly placed three counters on a 3 × 3 grid. Child 1 is asking questions to find out where the counters are. She has located one counter so far.

C1: *Two along and three down?*

T: You mean in the middle at the bottom?

C1: *Yes, in the middle at the bottom.*

C2: *No.*

(Child 2 looks around the screen to check which square Child 1 is describing.)

T: Is she close?

C2: *Yes!*

C1: *On the left at the bottom?*

C2: *Nearly.*

C1: *At the bottom on the right?*

C2: *Yes!*

(Child 1 places a counter in the bottom right square of her grid.)

C1: *Um, in the middle ... on the right?*

▲ Child 2 looks around the screen to check which square Child 1 is describing.

C2: *You already asked that!*

C1: *No, I didn't?*

T: Is there a way of recording where we've already tried? What could we use?

C2: *Counters?*

T: Is there anything you could do on the paper? Counters might get confusing.

C2: *Use a pencil?*

T: Yes, good. We can use a pencil to mark which ones we have already guessed. So, if it's right, put a counter down, and if not, we'll make a mark to say we've asked.

C1: *Is it the top on the right?*

C2: *No.*

(Child 1 marks the square with a pencil dot.)

> *Why is it useful to keep track of what we have already asked?*

▲ Support children to mark the squares they have already asked about so they don't keep asking about them.

T: Well done, so do we need to ask about that one again?

C1: *No.*

C2: *In the top on the left?*

What next?
Children play again and find a way to record how many turns it takes.

Needing support

Look and listen for children who do not use positional language to ask their questions, and revert to pointing to squares on the grid.

Child 1 is trying to guess the positions of Child 2's counters. He has found one so far, in the middle square. The teacher has made prompt cards (left, right, middle) to support Child 1 with language.

C1: This one?

(Child points to the top left square.)

T: What do you call that square? Is it the left, middle or right?

(Child looks unsure.)

T: It's tricky isn't it? This card says 'left'.

(Teacher holds up card with the word 'left'.)

T: Is this the r-r-right or the l-l-left?

(Teacher points to the left side of the board.)

C1: Left.

T: Good, so let's put this card there so that it matches up.

(Teacher places the card above the left-hand column.

T: Then you can see that that's the left, so whenever you want to describe it you know that that's the left.

(Teacher holds up card with the word 'right'.)

T: And this one says 'right'. Where would that one go? Can you put it in the correct place?

(Child places the card above the right-hand column.)

T: Well done. Can you use them to ask a question?

C1: On the left?

(Child points to the top left square.)

T: Let's have a look.

(Teacher holds up a card with the word 'middle', then places it to the left of the middle column.)

C1: Middle.

> Consider what language is familiar to children and what vocabulary they would be most comfortable using.

> Labelling helps reduce the amount of information the child is having to deal with.

▲ Consider if directional arrow labels would suit your children better than word labels.

T: So what's this one?

(Teacher points to the top left square.)

C1: Top.

T: We need a bit more information than that. Point to the square you want to ask about.

(Child points to the top left.)

T: Good, so if this is the middle (teacher indicates middle column), what would this be?

C1: Left.

T: Yes, it's left. But look, this one is the middle (teacher indicates middle row), so this one is the ...?

C1: Top.

T: Good. So, which square is this?

(Teacher points to the top left square.)

T: On the ...

C1: Top.

T: On the top, on the ...

C1: Left.

T: Well done. So is there a counter there?

C2: Yes.

T: Well done!

(Child 1 places a counter in the top left square.)

Which squares could be described by 'top'? Why do we need to give more information?

Would a sentence frame be helpful here?

What next?

Let children work in pairs (two either side of the screen), and ask them to rehearse their question with their partner before asking it.

Going deeper

Children play using a larger grid (e.g. 4 × 4). They will need to use more complex sentences and ordinal language, e.g. Is there a counter in the third square of the second row? They must make sure they are using the same language to describe the squares.

Child 2 has placed three counters on a 4 × 4 grid. Child 1 starts trying to locate them.

C1: At the top in the middle?

C2: Umm ...

T: Oh, that's hard isn't it? Now that it's a four by four grid, what's the middle?

C1: Hmm ... this is the left middle (child points to the second column) *and this is the right middle?* (Child points to the third column.)

> Moving from a 3 by 3 grid to 4 by 4 steps up the level of challenge.

◄ The teacher and children agree what to call the second and third columns and rows, now that 'middle' is not a clear enough description.

T: You could say that, couldn't you? Is there any other way you could describe the spaces? Do you remember your columns and rows?

C1: Yes?

T: So this could be called a column.

(Teacher indicates the left-hand column.)

   And what is this?

(Teacher indicates the top row.)

C2: Top.

T: Yes, it's the top row. So we have one, two, three, four columns.

(Teacher points to each column.)

   And one, two, three, four rows.

(Teacher points to each row.)

> The teacher begins, informally, to introduce the idea of coordinates.

T: So where is this?

(Teacher runs a finger down the second column.)

C2: Second ... column?

T: Yes, good. Now guess a space, but this time using columns and rows.

C1: Second column in the top row?

C2: No.

C1: Third row, first column?

C2: No.

T: Can you both point to the third row and the first column for me?

(Child 1 points to the first column, three rows down from the top. Child 2 points to the first column, three rows up from the bottom.)

> The teacher checks that both children are interpreting the terms in the same way.

T: Can you both point to the first row?

(Child 1 points to the top row. Child 2 points to the bottom row.)

T: That's interesting isn't it? So (Child 1) you've said that this is the first row (teacher points at top row), but (Child 2) you've said that this is the first row (teacher points at bottom row). Do you think that makes a difference to the game?

C1: Yes, because we're looking at different rows.

> *What would happen if we carried on using the language in different ways to each other?*

T: Right, so if you can't see each other's boards, do you think you need to use the same language?

Cs: Yes.

T: Good. So you two agree on how you're going to name the rows, then carry on.

What next?

Children work with a 5 × 5 grid and keep a running record of their guesses.

◀ A child celebrates locating a counter on the 5 × 5 grid.

Notes